Customizing Your Boat

Customizing Your Boat

Ian Nicolson FRINA

VAN NOSTRAND REINHOLD COMPANY

NEW YORK CINCINNATI TORONTO LONDON MELBOURNE

Originally published under the title *Marinize your Boat*
by Stanford Maritime Limited, 12-14 Long Acre, London
WC2E 9LP, England.

Published in 1975 by Van Nostrand Reinhold Company
A division of Litton Educational Publishing, Inc.
450 West 33rd Street, New York, NY 10001

16 15 14 13 12 11 10 9 8 7 6 5 4 3 2

Library of Congress Cataloging in Publication Data

Nicolson, Ian, 1928—
Customizing your boat.

1. Yachts and yachting. 2. Yacht-building.
3. Boats and boating. 4. Boat-building. I. Title.
VM331.N49   1975   623.82'2   75-12385
ISBN 0-442-26025-3

To Dick Hughes

Contents

Introduction

A single step leads down into the cabin of the boat I have just built for myself. The tread is of unvarnished teak because this wood is not slippery even when wet, and the drips through the companionway will not rot it. Also it looks smart. The side pieces are of a lovely creamy Honduras mahogany, a lightweight, easily worked wood. They are well polished to prevent water penetrating, and the weight saving will give my yacht that millionth of a knot extra. No mass produced boat could have such complexities as two different woods with different finishes within the compass of a single step. The sink cover is of teak also. It's an eighth of an inch too thick so that every few years I can plane off the surface, which doubles as a chopping board and gets marked with deep knife cuts. The screws which hold the tiepieces are just long enough to do the job, but short enough to avoid catching the plane blade if I cut away a little too much wood.

It is details like this that make my boat—or your boat—pleasant to own, a little bit safer and a tiny bit faster.

That is one aspect of this book: consolidated knowhow—small craft technology made easy to read and simple to apply. If a boat has a problem, there is a good chance that a solution lies within these pages. It may not be the precise answer, but it is likely to be enough to guide the owner or builder, or to suggest further ideas. Many problems are not new, and people from all over the world have invented, had brainwaves, been cunning, or applied a new idea to an old problem, or an old idea to a new one. Where an answer does not appear here, there is a fair chance that it is in the earlier companion volume *Designer's Notebook*.

The thousands of builders, draughtsmen, managers, moulders, riggers, welders, mast makers, sail makers and thoughtful amateurs who assemble, repair, sell and generally look fter boats are the people who have really written this book. I have not been able to give credit where it is due except in a few cases, because so often an idea emerges in several places at the same time.

Many of these sketches have appeared in *Yachts and Yachting* and I am indebted to that magazine for permission to reproduce them here.

Hull Construction

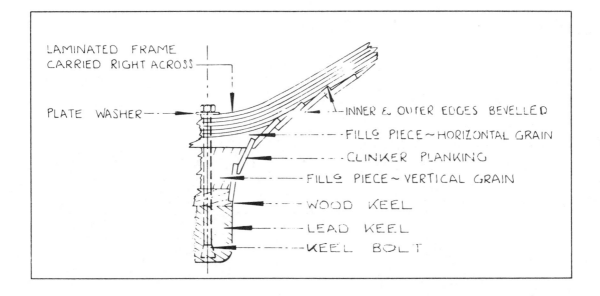

LAMINATED FRAME
CARRIED RIGHT ACROSS

PLATE WASHER

INNER & OUTER EDGES BEVELLED

FILLG PIECE~HORIZONTAL GRAIN

CLINKER PLANKING

FILLG PIECE~VERTICAL GRAIN

WOOD KEEL

LEAD KEEL

KEEL BOLT

Half and half   Traditional clinker planking
can be combined with modern laminated
methods. On this cruiser the frames are built up
from gunwale to gunwale and sweep across the
top of the keel. Alternate frames run down into
the keel and each plank is recessed into
individually-cut notches at every frame. As
a result the planks are very thoroughly supported
and well secured.

One of the attractions of using this type of
frame is that the glue line forms a water barrier
so that soakage is checked, and of course
there are no weak points caused by faults in the
wood.

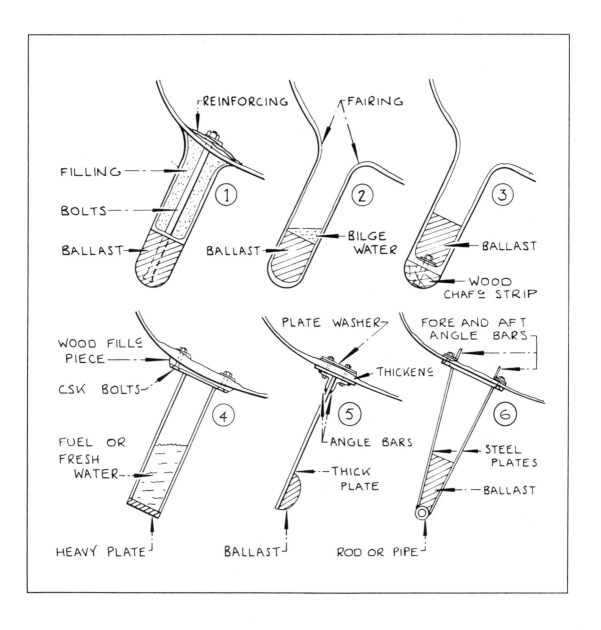

Bilge keels   There are various ways of
making twin fins. The series in the top row are
all moulded in fibreglass, with (1) added to the
hull after the main hull shell moulding has been
completed. The first three versions are all faired
into the main hull to ensure adequate strength.
Type (1) has the ballast bolted onto the outside,
which is an advantage in the event of grounding.
On the other hand keel bolts are a nuisance since
they rust, or if they are stainless steel they are
expensive and still sometimes corrode. An
alternative is to put the ballast inside the moulding as shown in (2), but when the yacht touches
the ground she is likely to chafe the fibreglass,
which can be serious. One way to prevent this
is to fit wood chafing strips along the bottom
edges of the fins (3). Where the fins are moulded
as part of the main hull, bilgewater is likely to
lie in them. It may be difficult to pump out
entirely ; on the other hand the last remaining
water should not slosh about under berths
and lockers and wet bedding and gear.

Type (4) is found on some production models
now being built. The fins are in the form of
shaped tanks which means that the fuel or
water are carried as low as possible. Type (5) is
probably the cheapest arrangement of all, but
is not very efficient hydrodynamically. The
angle-bars at the top are essential except on the
very smallest boats, otherwise the fins will tend
to bend at the roots. The internal plate washer
shown in this version is a very good idea since
it spreads the load on the hull shell. Type (6) is
even better in this respect since the loading is
spread both fore and aft by angle-bars and
athwartships by a big upper plate.

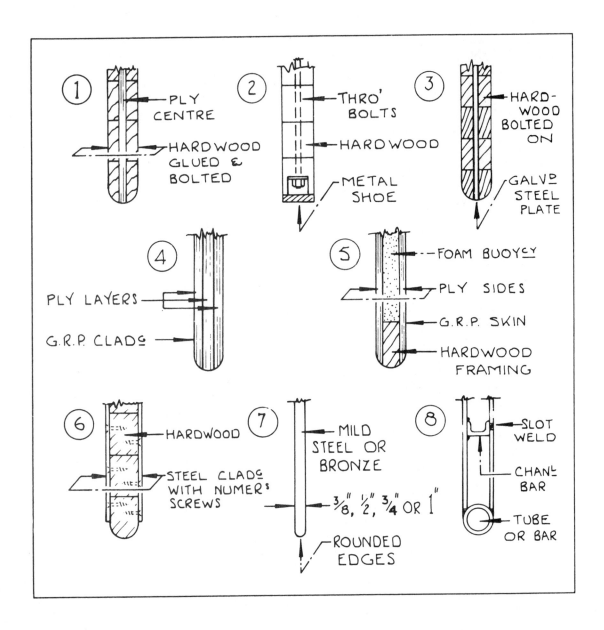

1 — PLY CENTRE / HARDWOOD GLUED & BOLTED

2 — THRO' BOLTS / HARDWOOD / METAL SHOE

3 — HARDWOOD BOLTED ON / GALVᴰ STEEL PLATE

4 — PLY LAYERS / G.R.P. CLADᵍ

5 — FOAM BUOYᶜʸ / PLY SIDES / G.R.P. SKIN / HARDWOOD FRAMING

6 — HARDWOOD / STEEL CLADᵍ WITH NUMERˢ SCREWS

7 — MILD STEEL OR BRONZE / ⅜", ½", ¾" OR 1" / ROUNDED EDGES

8 — SLOT WELD / CHANᴸ BAR / TUBE OR BAR

Cruiser centreboards   There are many ways of making a centreboard for a cruiser. However a hollow fibreglass envelope, possibly filled with foam plastic, is seldom rugged enough, and not able to take the frequent abrasion which occurs when the board touches bottom.

One of the simplest is shown in (1). Here the centreboard is cut out in plywood and sheathed on both sides with hardwood. This should be glued and through-bolted, or possibly clenched, to give a very rigid board. The advantages are low cost, ease of repair and ease of fabrication. (2) shows the traditional type of board, but it is getting harder to obtain suitable wood and drilling for the through-bolts is an awkward job. This type of board can be made self-sinking by fitting a heavy metal shoe whereas (1) will need some arrangement for forcing the board down.

Design (3) is a practical arrangement where a heavy board is required, but there are fabrication problems. The steel plate in the centre should be drilled before it is galvanized, and it is sometimes difficult to locate the holes when some of the wood cladding has been fitted. (4) can be made self-sinking by including a metal shoe either inside or outside the fibreglass skin. (5) is the lightest and in some ways the most sophisticated. Some form of tackle is needed to force the board down since this type will float. The sixth is good in that no bolts are required. However a great many countersunk screws are required and this type is not as easy to make as it first seems. Again, the steel plates must be galvanized after drilling.

Very expensive boats sometimes have bronze plates, as shown in (7). Mild steel plates are also used, but it is important to have them thick enough otherwise they will bend and jam in the casing. (8) has a number of attractive features: it is hard wearing yet not too heavy; it will also tend to sink under most conditions and needs only an uphaul tackle, whereas a section like (5) needs both an uphaul and a downhaul.

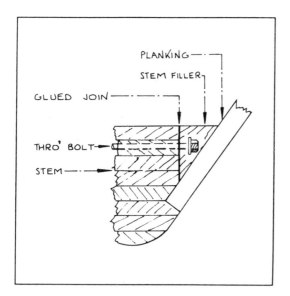

Extended stem   A stem piece which is adequate in width at its top may be too small lower down. Where it grows into the keel the planking joins it at a flatter angle so that there may not be enough 'meat' to hold the fastenings. In this case cheek pieces on each side of the stem are needed. They should be put in before planking up and faired into the stem after gluing and bolting. Their extent can be discerned on the mould loft floor, but an inexperienced shipwright would probably be advised to wait until the backbone is erected before adding the cheek pieces. Just occasionally these side fillers are put in for no other reason than to bridge the hollow each side of the stem. This is done by top builders when the yacht has an open plan layout where the inside of the stem will be seen.

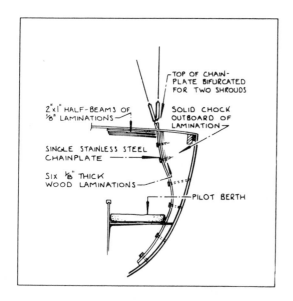

Chainplate support   On an amateur designed and built 35 ft ocean racer the single chainplate on each side was fitted to a massive wood chock to provide a really reliable fixing. On the inboard side there are multiple thin laminations, like the beam laminations. The shroud stresses are thereby carried down below the bilge.

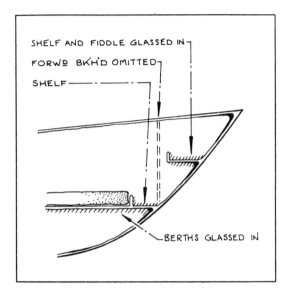

SHELF AND FIDDLE GLASSED IN

FORWᴰ BK'H'D OMITTED

SHELF

BERTHS GLASSED IN

Bows without bulkheads A successful way to make the inside of a yacht seem bigger is to leave out bulkheads and lockers. An illusion of space is given because the eye looks into relatively distant, dim corners. A good instance is right forward, where the bulkhead may be omitted, to leave the interior open right up to the inside face of the stem.

As the forward bulkhead often has to work as part of the hull structure, it cannot be left out without compensating stiffening being put in. This can take the form of a shelf which, even with a fiddle, does not limit the length of forward vision. Naturally nothing heavy should be loaded into this shelf when speed is the aim. The forward berth bottom can also be glassed in to give the bows strength, again without detracting from appearance.

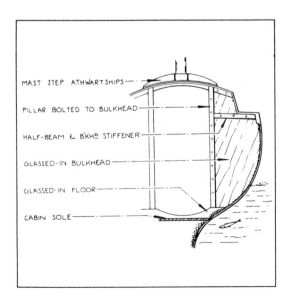

MAST STEP ATHWARTSHIPS

PILLAR BOLTED TO BULKHEAD

HALF-BEAM & B'KHᴰ STIFFENER

GLASSED-IN BULKHEAD

GLASSED-IN FLOOR

CABIN SOLE

Beefing up the mast supports If a boat is found to work in way of the mast it is essential to stiffen the structure. Signs of movement include hair cracks where beams join decking or at bulkhead edges, doors that shut well on moorings but jam under way, and suspiciously slack rigging. Plenty of cruisers are built to an economical specification for inshore or estuary sailing, but their owners may find themselves in conditions that have not been designed for, or want to venture further afield.

A deck-stepped mast arrangement can often be strengthened with little hull work, simply by altering the step or tabernacle. A wide, deep steel step spreads the load athwartships, which cures much of the trouble emanating from over-flexible beams. It can be made to straddle two pillars, as shown, acting as a beam in transferring the mast load to the vertical supports. Pillars are fairly easily added or altered by stiffening or replacing with larger scantlings. Cross pieces through-fastened at close intervals to the bulkhead help to stiffen both it and the pillars and to link the structure to the side decks. Additional glassing-in on both sides of the bulkhead and floors is normally straightforward.

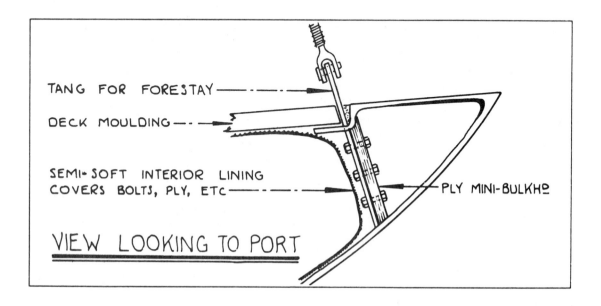

TANG FOR FORESTAY

DECK MOULDING

SEMI-SOFT INTERIOR LINING
COVERS BOLTS, PLY, ETC

PLY MINI-BULKHD

VIEW LOOKING TO PORT

Headstay tang   It is difficult to join a metal rigging tang to relatively brittle fibreglass and ensure that the fastenings do not cause local cracking. Many GRP cruisers thus have heavy and sometimes rather ugly stem fittings for the purpose, but a recently designed 30 ft production cruiser has a miniature bulkhead worked in right forward to which the tang is bolted. The bulkhead is glassed in all round and the extreme forward end of the deck is glassed over it. Stay loads are thus distributed between the deck and hull rather than concentrated at one or two small areas, and as the deck is restrained from lifting stress on the crucial hull/deck join is reduced. The main deck moulding rests on a ledge formed by an athwartships flange which strengthens the end of the deck in way of the tang.

Bracing an anchor winch   It is not unusual to moor onto the anchor winch, yet this fitting is normally located on the centreline, often far from any strong structural member. The larger sketch shows some of the techniques which can be used to ensure that the winch does not tear off the deck. It is mounted on an extra long pad which is not only bolted through the deck, but is extended aft and bolted through a beam which in turn is secured strongly to a strength bulkhead. Such bulkheads are secured top, bottom and down both sides, and do not have too much cut away in the middle for the access door.

The bottom of the bulkhead is secured to a floor, and growing up from this is a tube which is welded to plates at each end. The upper plate is bolted to another strong beam which takes the winch foot bolts. One advantage of using a tube here is that it will stand both compression and tension. It must, of course, be angled aft if it is to be fully effective, but even a

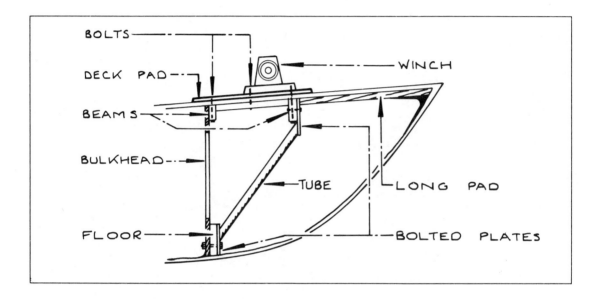

vertical pillar can contribute something to the general strength of structure. To help deal with the forward pull there is a long pad extending under the deck from the winch right to the stem. This must be fitted tightly and well secured if it is to be any good.

The smaller drawing shows a winch added to a boat of about 25 ft overall. First, a full length underdeck pad has been glassed in right up to the stem. Next a pad has been put on deck, made long partly to enable plenty of fastenings to pass through to the lower pad, partly to protect the deck from the chafe of the mud-laden chain. Both pads are bolted to a beam secured to the forward bulkhead which in turn is given extra glassing all round the forward and aft edges. Some vertical stiffening and possibly horizontal stiffening at one-third and two-thirds height may be advisable if the bulkhead is a flimsy one.

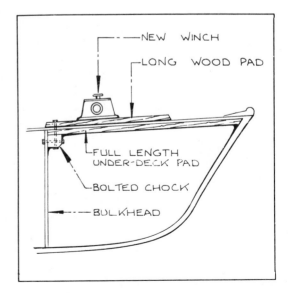

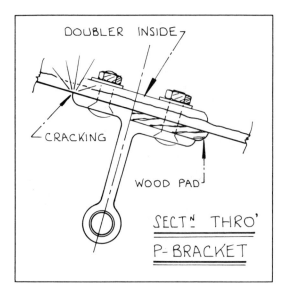

DOUBLER INSIDE

CRACKING

WOOD PAD

SECT<u>N</u> THRO'
P-BRACKET

Hull-cracker   The bracket which supports a propeller shaft should not be bolted directly to a fibreglass hull because it is likely to cause cracking round the edge of the flange. This is particularly likely if the engine vibrates a great deal or if the prop tip touches something solid like driftwood or the seabed.

A wood pad greatly reduces the risk of this trouble, and incidentally makes it easy to get correct alignment of the bearing. If the P-bracket is fitted direct to the hull with no pad, it is all too likely that the hull is not exactly in the same plane as the bracket palm. This discrepancy may be made up by the hull flexing when the bolts are drawn tight and then cracking is all the more certain. To allow the water to flow over the pad and palm easily, the pad should extend well fore and aft and be tapered when clear of the palm.

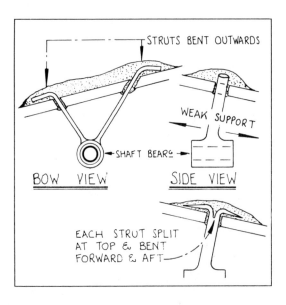

STRUTS BENT OUTWARDS

WEAK SUPPORT

SHAFT BEAR<u>G</u>

BOW VIEW   SIDE VIEW

EACH STRUT SPLIT
AT TOP & BENT
FORWARD & AFT

Strong strut   The top two sketches show an arrangement used on some fibreglass boats for securing the propeller shaft A-bracket. The arms of the bracket are passed through the hull and bent outwards, then glassed over. The arms are narrow in a fore-and-aft direction, so until the shaft has been fitted any bump against the A-bracket on the forward or aft face meets little resistance. Since boats have to be moved about during construction and the A-bracket stands out from the hull, the chances of cracking the inner fibreglass doubling are high. The trouble can be resolved by splitting each arm of the A-bracket at the top and bending the ends in a fore-and-aft direction. The bedded-in parts should have no sharp corners and should taper away to give the strongest join.

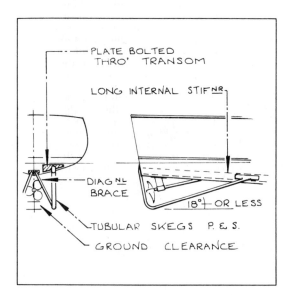

PLATE BOLTED
THRO' TRANSOM

LONG INTERNAL STIF^NR

DIAG^NL
BRACE

18° + OR LESS

TUBULAR SKEGS P. & S.

GROUND CLEARANCE

Prop guard   A boat operating in shallow water may run aground many times with impunity, then one day be unlucky and damage her propeller. If it is just a nick or two on the blade edges the boat can go on working, perhaps running a little slower. But if she crumples a blade she is likely to be out of action for some time, and costs and bad tempers escalate.

Twin skegs made of tubing are not too hard to fit, provided there is adequate internal strengthening. The forward arms should if possible subtend an angle of 18° or less to the horizontal to avoid excessive water resistance. The aft arms will normally bolt to broad plates on the transom so that the load is well spread. This idea is good for boats up to about 35 ft overall, but thereafter the stresses tend to be frightening.

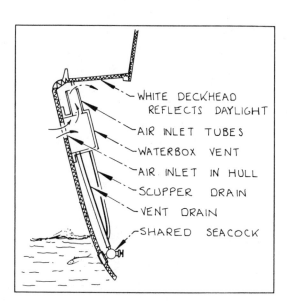

WHITE DECKHEAD
REFLECTS DAYLIGHT

AIR INLET TUBES

WATERBOX VENT

AIR INLET IN HULL

SCUPPER DRAIN

VENT DRAIN

SHARED SEACOCK

Light and air   On a powered vessel it is important to get plenty of air into the engine compartment. At the same time many people prefer clear decks, and ventilators working through the topsides have many assets. The ventilator shown consists of a rectangular box with a flange secured to the topsides and wide air inlet tubes extending up near the deckhead. Spray drains out through a seacock which also serves the scupper drains. This largely eliminates water stains on the topsides.

Daylight comes in through the hole in the topsides and will be reflected off the deckhead if this is painted white. Even more effective is to make the whole vent of translucent fibreglass, which should be about half as effective as a clear port. If a female mould is used the smooth side will be visible when fitted, and the vent can be reasonably attractive as well as useful.

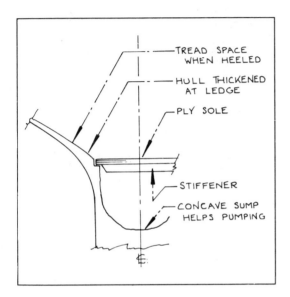

TREAD SPACE WHEN HEELED

HULL THICKENED AT LEDGE

PLY SOLE

STIFFENER

CONCAVE SUMP HELPS PUMPING

Narrow sole   When designing a fibreglass boat it is common sense to get the maximum advantage out of the material. There are no frames and there should seldom be water inside the boat, so there is no reason why the sole should not be low down and set onto the inner face of the hull shell. The technique shown is for small yachts, say under 30 ft. There must be some building up of the shell in the area of the ledge to take the sole, so that there is reserve strength to cope with the clumping about of heavy-footed crews. Provided the sole is narrow and the ply from which it is made is fairly thick, no athwartships bearers are needed. If the ply tends to bend it can be made rigid by stiffeners glued to the under side.

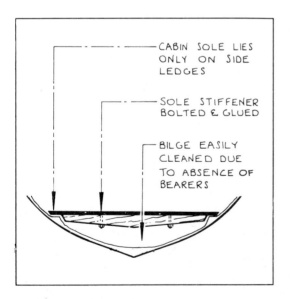

CABIN SOLE LIES ONLY ON SIDE LEDGES

SOLE STIFFENER BOLTED & GLUED

BILGE EASILY CLEANED DUE TO ABSENCE OF BEARERS

Wider sole   Here the hull shape is flatter and the sole has to span a wider gap. This shape is likely to be seen on bilge-keelers and on some modern fin-keelers. Although the sole is supported in the same way, on a short, thick ledge moulded into the hull shell, it requires stiffening, particularly in the middle. It is still easily removed for inspection or cleaning, and unlikely to bind on the hull.

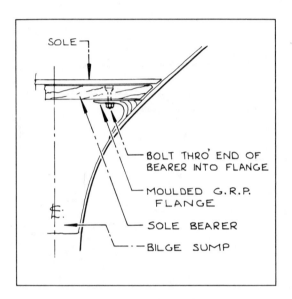

SOLE

BOLT THRO' END OF
BEARER INTO FLANGE

MOULDED G.R.P.
FLANGE

SOLE BEARER

BILGE SUMP

Sole flange   The bilge in this 35 ft fibre-glass offshore yacht is deep under the saloon floor, and unless there is a lot of water on board the moulded flange will tend to keep it from slopping up into the accommodation when the boat is heeling. It also acts as a continuous longitudinal stiffener for the lower part of the hull. The section shown is of the aft end of the saloon.

BILGE WATER SUMP

EDGES OF FILLER
SWEPT UP

Bilge lining   Steel hulls are sometimes built with deep fins which are filled with chunks of ballast. Once all the ballast has been firmly wedged in place, pitch or concrete is poured in to seal the top. The sealing should be swept up at each side and a central indentation left. As puddles lie in the bilge even with the best pumping system, the aim must be to keep the puddles lying on the filler and not touching the steel. If moisture is in long-term contact with the steel just at the top of the ballast, this area is likely to corrode. This can be an expensive problem because the corrosion sometimes extends the full length of the ballast top and the replacement plates may need considerable shaping. Also, replacing the fin plating normally means taking out all the ballast, which will involve supporting the hull at each bilge while keel repairs are carried out, and this can be difficult.

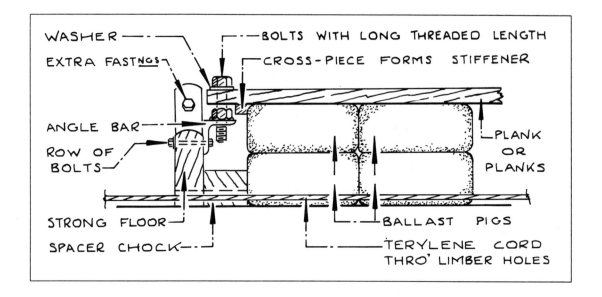

WASHER — · — —BOLTS WITH LONG THREADED LENGTH
EXTRA FAST**NOS** —CROSS-PIECE FORMS STIFFENER

ANGLE BAR — · —   PLANK
ROW OF   OR
BOLTS   PLANKS

STRONG FLOOR
SPACER CHOCK — · —   — · — BALLAST PIGS
                                      TERYLENE CORD
                                      THRO' LIMBER HOLES

Securing ballast   When the weather turns truly vicious and boats are turned upside down, it's no fun to have the internal ballast roaming about inside the hull. Yet it is not easy to secure iron or lead pigs. The common way, using wood wedges, has a host of disadvantages; for instance the wedges shrink when dry and become loose. This happens below the floorboards and so is likely to go unnoticed until the ballast emerges from its den and rampages about unchecked.

The technique suggested here is to first stiffen the floors, then bolt angle bars to them. Some stout boards are laid over the ballast and holes drilled through their ends and down through the angle bars. The latter holes are enlarged, then nuts are welded over them. Bolts through the cover boards engage in the welded nuts. Another approach is to have thicker bars and tap them instead of welding on nuts. The top boards are stiffened by wood straps athwartships on the under side which also prevent the ballast moving fore and aft.

The Terylene (Dacron) cord through the limber holes is to keep a free passage for bilgewater. It is pulled back and forth once a week to displace dirt and rust which blocks the holes.

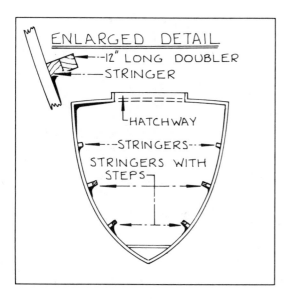

Simple steps This idea was seen on a 35 ft catamaran but it is applicable to many multihulls and might be suitable for some monohulls. Instead of fitting a ladder from the hatchway down to the sole the stringers are doubled in width to turn them into steps. The stringers themselves are full length and are strongly secured, so they are rigid enough to support a heavy man's weight. The steps are made by gluing and screwing additional lengths of stringer on the inside. It may be necessary to put two lengths of doubler on the inside, and possibly beef up the stringer locally. Of course these steps are not sufficiently convenient for use as a main cabin access, but they suit a forward or aft hatch which is used only occasionally.

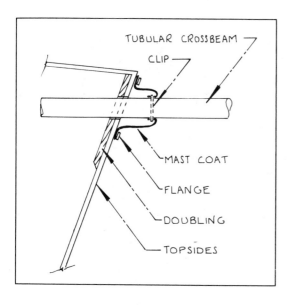

Watertight crossbeam seals On cats and tris which are held together by tubular cross-beams there is a danger zone where these tubes enter the topsides. There is considerable strain on this area and leaks are all too likely. Probably the best way of ensuring that water is kept out is to make an oversize hole for the tube and seal it with a flexible rubber skirt, in fact a mast coat. As one-piece mast coats are available from mast makers there is no difficulty in obtaining all the necessary fittings including stainless steel clamps which secure the rubber to the tube. For deep sea work it might be worth fitting an inner and outer mast coat as a double precaution. The flange which holds the wide edge of the coat to the hull should be through-bolted or screwed down at close intervals and very well bedded down.

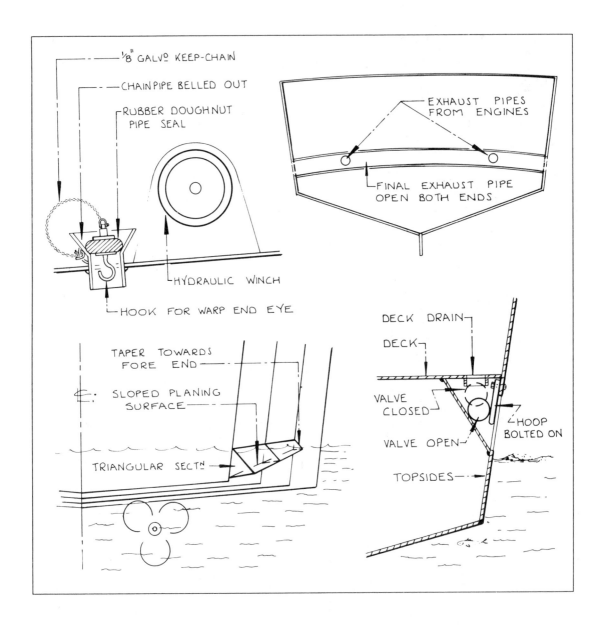

⅛" GALVᴰ KEEP-CHAIN

CHAINPIPE BELLED OUT

RUBBER DOUGHNUT
PIPE SEAL

HYDRAULIC WINCH

HOOK FOR WARP END EYE

EXHAUST PIPES
FROM ENGINES

FINAL EXHAUST PIPE
OPEN BOTH ENDS

TAPER TOWARDS
FORE END

SLOPED PLANING
SURFACE

TRIANGULAR SECTᴺ

DECK DRAIN

DECK

VALVE
CLOSED

VALVE OPEN

TOPSIDES

HOOP
BOLTED ON

Steel design   The hull of the recently built fast RNLI lifeboat *Connel Elizabeth Cargill* has a number of ingenious aspects, including those shown here. To save weight she carries an anchor warp instead of chain. The pipe through the deck for this warp has a wide mouth to ensure that it runs out freely without chafing, and a rubber 'doughnut' which seals the pipe. Both ideas are applicable to yachts.

The engine exhausts discharge into an athwartships pipe of considerably greater diameter which extends across the hull and is open at both ends. In rough seas or when rolling there is less back-pressure from the exhaust outlets being immersed. When both sides are very temporarily under waves the exhaust gases can still expand into the larger pipe. A second advantage is that the exhaust is blown off to leeward and is less likely to waft back aboard over the stern.

At the waterline and below there are steel sponsons running aft to the transom. They give additional planing surface, and because they are angled upwards they tend to lift the stern at speed and affect trim. Coincidentally they also stiffen the plating aft.

Very simple, ingenious non-return valves prevent the deck being flooded. Recesses in the topsides are welded in up to the deck. A short length of pipe down from the deck takes the water away quickly because it has a diameter of about 3 in, unlike so many inadequate small craft drains. A simple plastic ball forms the valve and is held in place by a semi-portable hoop bolted to the topsides. As a wave tries to flood back up through the drain the ball floats upwards and blocks the deck outlet.

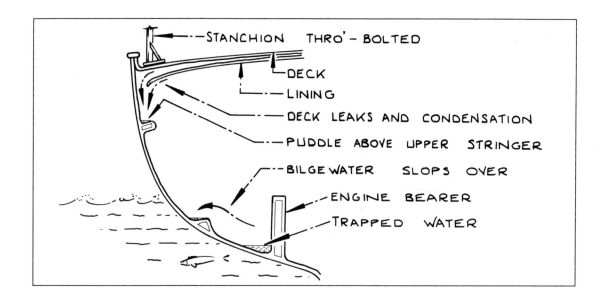

- STANCHION THRO'- BOLTED
- DECK
- LINING
- DECK LEAKS AND CONDENSATION
- PUDDLE ABOVE UPPER STRINGER
- BILGE WATER SLOPS OVER
- ENGINE BEARER
- TRAPPED WATER

Puddle catchers   It is very nearly impossible to stop water getting inside a boat and even the most watertight fibreglass shell often has puddles of moisture inside it. Water gets in through hatches, down chainpipes, and surprisingly often via the stanchion holding-down bolts. In addition there is condensation which is likely to collect on any shiny surface.

Water accumulates on top of stringers and for this reason it is worth fitting the stringers so that they run diagonally down into the bilge. If upper stringers are made triangular in section then water cannot lodge on the upper surface, but triangular section stringers low down catch and hold puddles of bilgewater in areas where the pump suction cannot reach. Sometimes it is possible to put the stringers in discontinuously, with breaks to let the water drop through. To keep the overall strength of the boat there must be what are in effect butt straps—short lengths of stringer set an inch or two above or below the main lengths of stringer. Enclosed areas such as those along engine bearers should be drained with non-ferrous tubes leading through the bearers, or there should be arrangements for draining the water away at one end.

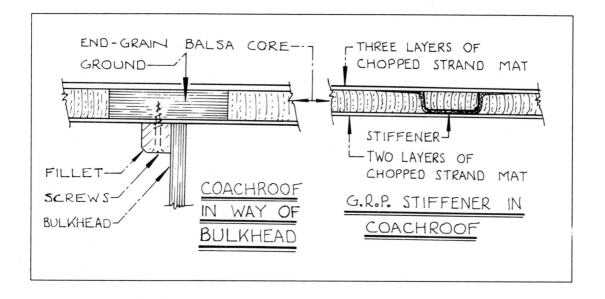

END-GRAIN BALSA CORE

GROUND

THREE LAYERS OF CHOPPED STRAND MAT

FILLET

SCREWS

BULKHEAD

COACHROOF IN WAY OF BULKHEAD

STIFFENER

TWO LAYERS OF CHOPPED STRAND MAT

G.R.P. STIFFENER IN COACHROOF

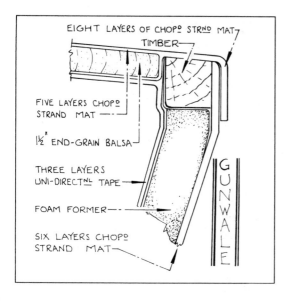

EIGHT LAYERS OF CHOPD STRND MAT

TIMBER

FIVE LAYERS CHOPD STRAND MAT

1½" END-GRAIN BALSA

THREE LAYERS UNI-DIRECTNL TAPE

FOAM FORMER

SIX LAYERS CHOPD STRAND MAT

GUNWALE

Heavy-duty fibreglass These details relate to the Halmatic 64 ft motor yacht hulls. Wide use is made of end-grain balsa for sandwich core material because it is found to be more reliable than many other materials which, although they may be lighter, are more prone to crushing and less effective in adhering to the inner and outer fibreglass layers. The internal ground (top left) is to prevent the coachroof from kinking or bulging in way of the bulkhead and to give a landing for the fillet screws. A simple and effective stiffener which can be built in at whatever spacing is required is shown top right.

The deck edge (bottom right) has ample stiffness contributed to by a timber strength member which also acts as a spacer between the inner and outer layers of fibreglass. The multiple layering of the deck edge is of interest because this is where poorly built fibreglass boats work and start to leak.

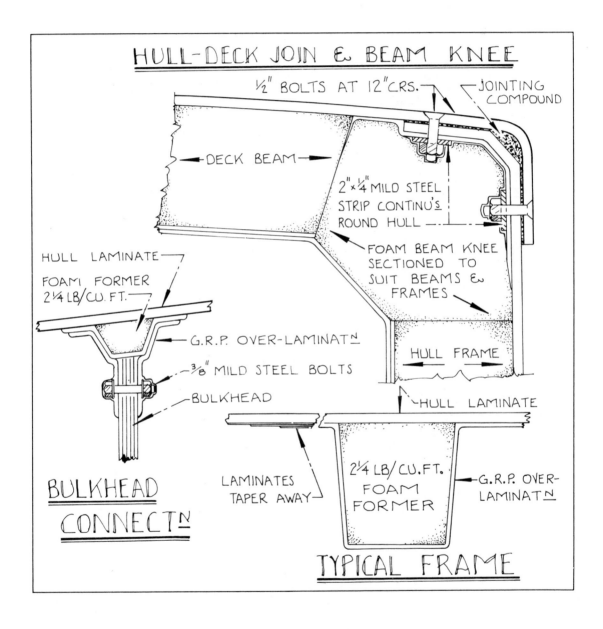

HULL-DECK JOIN & BEAM KNEE

½" BOLTS AT 12" CRS.

JOINTING COMPOUND

←DECK BEAM→

2" x ¼" MILD STEEL STRIP CONTINU'S ROUND HULL

FOAM BEAM KNEE SECTIONED TO SUIT BEAMS & FRAMES

HULL LAMINATE

FOAM FORMER 2¼ LB/CU.FT.

G.R.P. OVER-LAMINAT'N

HULL FRAME

⅜" MILD STEEL BOLTS

BULKHEAD

HULL LAMINATE

BULKHEAD CONNECT'N

LAMINATES TAPER AWAY

2¼ LB/CU.FT. FOAM FORMER

G.R.P. OVER-LAMINAT'N

TYPICAL FRAME

GRP construction   Here a return flange on
the hull fits under a vertical deck flange. Not
only are there two rows of bolts pulling the
deck tightly down on the hull, there is also a
very wide strip of jointing compound which is
compressed along both edges. To simplify construction the deck beam section is the same as
the hull frame section. Among its virtues are
light weight and adaptability ; for instance it
can be angled to miss ports, used on transoms,
and so on.

A typical bulkhead edge is detailed below.
The landing of the bulkhead is spread out to
avoid a sharp high-stress line on the hull, and
the combination of fibreglass and a row of
bolts gives belt-and-braces security. The foam
former has a tapered section similar to the
frame formers.

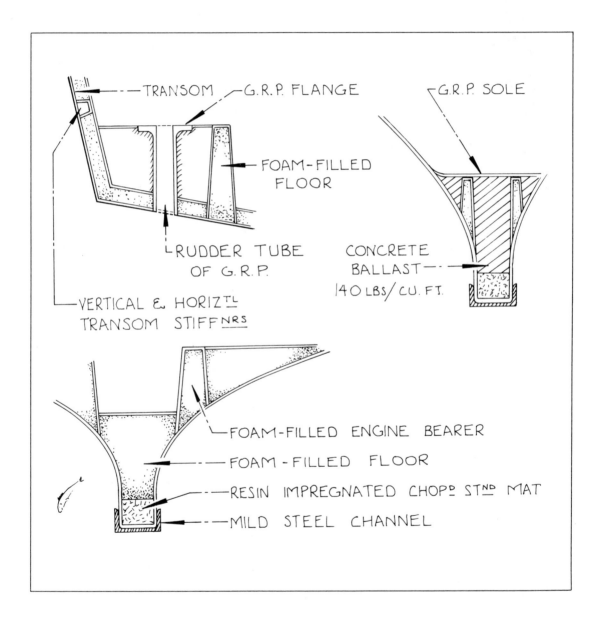

Trawler hull   These sketches show the way
Halmatic put together their 54 ft fibreglass
trawler hulls, though many of the features
detailed here are common to their other mouldings. For instance, they favour a simple,
reliable type of fibreglass rudder tube with an
integral top flange, made up on a mandrel and
glassed in with fore-and-aft and athwartships
stiffening. The transom and shell are reinforced
with tapered section stiffeners running vertically
and longitudinally. These are foam filled and
have the subsidiary advantage that localized
damage which does not extend beyond the area
of the stiffener will not let water in as long as
the foam remains intact.

The bottom has a filling of concrete ballast
sealed over with a fibreglass sole which is easy
to keep clean and impervious to water. The lower
part of the keel (bottom sketch) is reinforced
with a mild steel channel and a 4 in deep
length of resin-impregnated chopped strand
mat. The engine bearers are similar to the
stringers and frames, being foam-filled, tapered
fibreglass mouldings.

Deck Construction

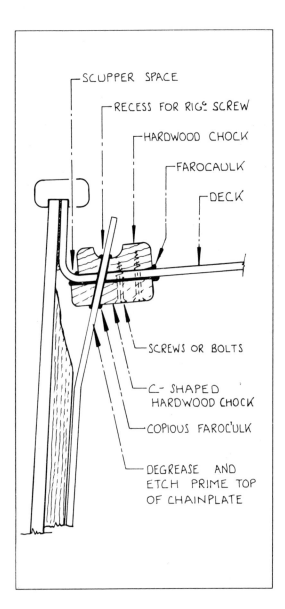

SCUPPER SPACE

RECESS FOR RIG: SCREW

HARDWOOD CHOCK

FAROCAULK

DECK

SCREWS OR BOLTS

C- SHAPED HARDWOOD CHOCK

COPIOUS FAROC'ULK

DEGREASE AND ETCH PRIME TOP OF CHAINPLATE

Chainplate leaks   The very high stresses put on a chainplate often result in leaks where the metal strap passes through the deck. A fibreglass deck is not easy to seal tightly around the metal, and may crack if the chainplate is not fitted exactly in line with the pull of the shroud.

Shown here is a technique for curing these deck leaks using two wood chocks and a plentiful supply of flexible, non-hardening sealant such as Farocaulk. The upper chock is made about four times the fore-and-aft width of the chainplate and as deep as possible consistent with clearing the rigging screw. The chocks will probably need gouging out to make room for the rigging screw end and should be fitted fairly tightly over the chainplate by cutting a slot in the wood of almost exactly the same size as the chainplate. The chock on the underside cannot be slipped on over the strap in the same way and so is made with an open-ended slot and slid into position, embracing the chainplate as closely as possible. The chainplate must be treated with a degreasing agent and then etch-primed to roughen the surface; this helps the sealant to stick. It is applied on top and underneath, then the two chocks are pushed into place and pulled tightly together with bolts or screws. Four or even six fastenings should be used to grip the two chocks tightly together through the deck. The sealant should squeeze out all round to show that plenty has been used.

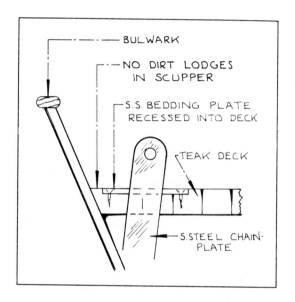

Clean decks   Teak decks do need attention every weekend and it is not easy to keep them clean if there are numerous little crannies where dirt can lodge. Scrubbing and draining are easier where the chainplates are slightly inboard of the bulwarks or toerail. The metal plate round each chainplate has been recessed here, so any water running towards the scuppers has an unimpeded path and will take dirt with it.

With this type of recessed plate leaks around the chainplates, if they do occur, are fairly easy to cure simply by lifting the plate, replacing the bedding material, and refastening.

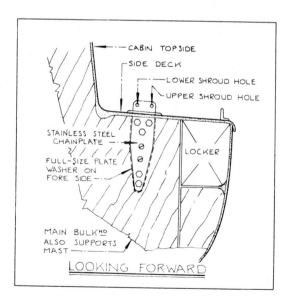

Inboard chainplates   On a 27-footer the chainplates were set well inboard, to make close sheeting easier, and in this case are far enough in so that the crew pass outside of them when moving along the deck. There are multiple bolts holding the plate to a strength bulkhead which also supports the mast and ties the deck and hull together. This type of chainplate is particularly attractive in that it is accessible rather than buried in fibreglass, and can be repaired.

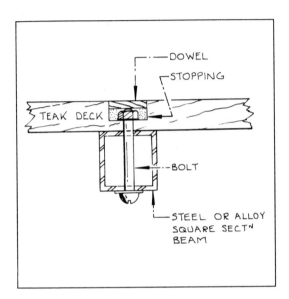

Tubular beams   Both steel and aluminium are available in the form of rectangular and square section tubing. Beams made of these sections have several advantages, including a good strength/weight ratio and neat appearance, and they may be used to carry electric cables. In both aluminium and steel there are a wide variety of sections available, and standard steel sections are made in more than one wall thickness for each external size.

The deck will normally be bolted down, care being taken to use sufficient thickness of wood to allow a proper length of dowel. Shallow dowels, even when glued in place, are all too vulnerable. They come out leaving awkward ugly holes in the deck which hold puddles every time spray or rain comes aboard.

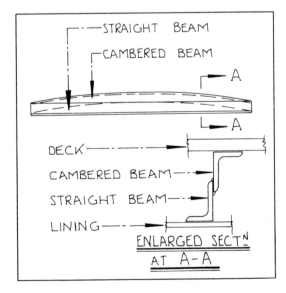

Composite beam   Building in either steel or aluminium, this technique can be used to simplify some construction problems. Normally the beam scantlings must be bigger than the frame scantlings, but by using two back-to-back angle-bars, beams can be made up from the same material as that used for frames. This simplifies ordering materials and can reduce costs by avoiding small quantities.

In addition, rolling the beams is made easier since only the relatively light top angle-bar is rolled, the bottom one being left straight. This in turn simplifies fitting the lining because it has no camber. The two bars are normally welded back to back but could be riveted provided there is overlap over the whole length so that the rivets are continuous right across the ship. The maximum depth of the cambered beam section is on the centreline just where the greatest strength is needed.

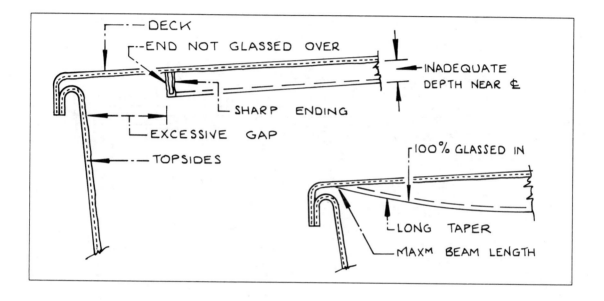

Fibreglass beams The left-hand sketch shows some of the cardinal sins which can be committed when putting in beams under a fibreglass deck. There is a temptation to make the beams very shallow so as to maintain maximum headroom, but if the deck is flexy the boat will have a short, sordid life. Ending a beam abruptly will result in a line of weakness extending from beam end to beam end, where gel coat cracks will appear. This is likely to be followed by water seepage, leaks and sundry other troubles. The right-hand drawing indicates the way beams should be fabricated, using common engineering principles. The taper, which is both long and close to the deck edge eliminates hard spots and unsupported panels besides sealing off the beam end. Electric cables can still be run inside the beam, but where they emerge the hole should be fully sealed with resin.

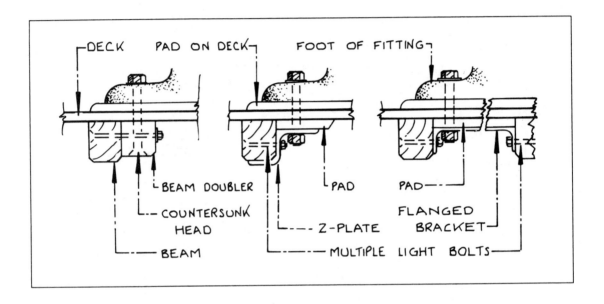

Securing deck fittings   On a wooden yacht it is often necessary to change or add to the fittings on deck. Often it is not practical to drill through the beams ; for instance, the bolts through the deck fittings may be too large for the beams and a hole big enough for a through-bolt would seriously weaken the beam. Or the beam does not come in just the right place for the holding-down bolts.

Sketched here are three techniques for getting round these problems. On the left, a doubler has been bolted to the beam using relatively light but numerous horizontal bolts. The vertical bolts through the fitting have the nuts on top so that there are no dangerous projections below the beam.

In the second sketch a Z-bar has been used. This can either be made up by welding or possibly flanging, or may be a standard section steel, aluminium or brass. Here the nut on the holding-down bolt is raised well above the underside of the beam.

The right hand sketch shows a neat way of dealing with the problem by fitting a flange bracket from beam to beam. Naturally the fit must be good, although even here packing pieces can be used between the faces of the beams and the vertical flanges.

In the second and third sketches an underdeck pad is shown, necessary partly to spread the load and partly to prevent the metal plate or bracket crushing the underside of the deck. It also serves to take up any 'want' between the metal and the deck.

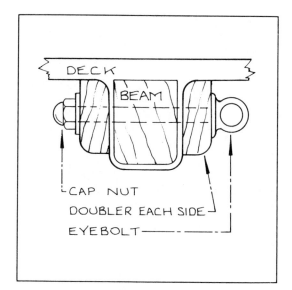

Securing an eyebolt   It is sometimes necessary to use an eyebolt instead of an eyeplate for holding up a leeboard or a cot berth. This use of a single fastening with an eye on the end tends to be bad practice, but there are occasions when it cannot be avoided. It is in general not a good idea to put an eyebolt like this through the deck because sooner or later it is likely to start leaks. On the other hand if it is put in horizontally (as shown), unless the work is done with forethought the beam will split with the sideways pull on the bolt. The first thing to do is double up the beam: the doublers should extend well beyond the actual fastening, and 8 in either side of a $\frac{3}{8}$ in diameter eyebolt is not too much. The doublers will need two screws at each end, as well as glue.

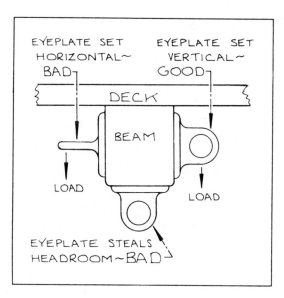

Leeboard eyeplate   Three ways of fitting an eyeplate to a beam are shown here. The one on the left is wrong because it imposes an unnecessarily high strain on the fastenings and also on the root of the eye where it joins its baseplate. In addition it may be difficult to clip a shackle into the eye because of the lack of space between the deckhead and the ring. The arrangement on the right is the correct one. Here the load comes as close to the beam as possible so that the strain on the fastenings is minimized. The fastenings are in their most effective position in relation to the pull, and the eye is placed so that there is the maximum amount of metal in line with the pull. Different types of shackles can be engaged in the eye without any difficulty and the eyeplate is as unobtrusive as possible. Putting an eyeplate on the bottom of a beam, as shown, is not good practice even when there is ample headroom.

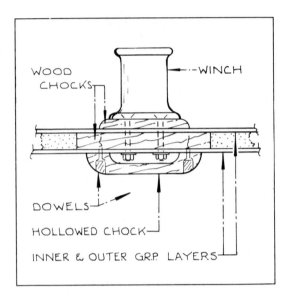

Foam sandwich fastening   In way of the winch there is the usual wood pad on top of the deck, and a wider pad between the two deck surfaces to prevent it from being squeezed when the bolts are tightened, and to spread the stresses. During construction of the hull and deck it is very important to mark the position and exact area of these solid chocks. They are sometimes made of marine plywood on the principle that if water does leak through via the fastening holes, ply soaks up very little due to its layers of glue.

In this example the nuts on the underside have been neatly concealed by a teak pad which has been machined out on the inside and screwed to the inner chock.

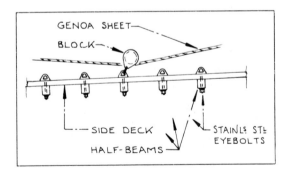

No sheet track   The conventional way to arrange adjustable genoa sheet leads is to have stainless steel tracks along either sidedeck. On each track there are one or two strong sliders with eyes on top for the shackles which hold the lead blocks.

This alternative is occasionally seen when the aim is to save weight, or when modifying an older boat. It saves money as well. Separate stainless steel eyebolts are used, one at each beam. If snatch-blocks are used the sheet can be snapped into a second block before being released from the first. Alternatively the port sheet and its block can be brought round to the starboard side and rove off at a new eye when the lead needs shifting. The bolt part of the eye is equivalent to the bolts in a track, so the weight saved is almost the whole weight of the tracks.

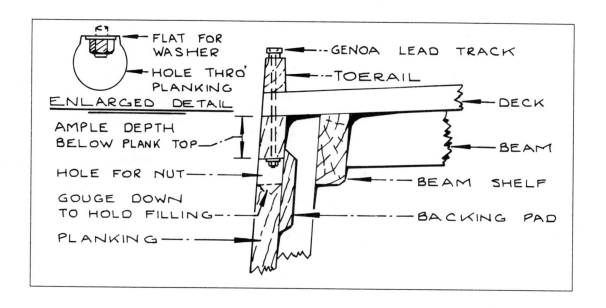

FLAT FOR WASHER

HOLE THRO' PLANKING

ENLARGED DETAIL

GENOA LEAD TRACK

TOERAIL

DECK

AMPLE DEPTH BELOW PLANK TOP

BEAM

HOLE FOR NUT

BEAM SHELF

GOUGE DOWN TO HOLD FILLING

BACKING PAD

PLANKING

Genoa lead track on a wooden yacht

It has always been difficult to secure a genoa sheet lead track right down at the very edge of a deck. On wooden yachts it has been common practice to put long screws down through the toerail, through the deck and into the hull planking. But screws are never entirely satisfactory, particularly if the shipwright makes a slight error and uses an oversized drill. If he uses an undersize drill and too much force on the screwdriver he may break the screws.

One trick is to use bolts which have nuts recessed into the planking. This is a time-consuming job which calls for great care, but makes good sense since it does give a high standard of reliability. Consideration might be given to fitting alternate bolts and screws, or even one bolt for every two screws. The recess for the nut can be made by drilling a hole right through the planking, clear of the frames, and then squaring the top of the hole so that the washer and nut lie on a flat surface. Skilled shipwrights sometimes use this technique but without going *right* through the planking. They chisel out a recess just deep enough to take the nut, but this is a tricky business and it is easy to make one or two mistakes when doing a whole row of bolts each side of the boat.

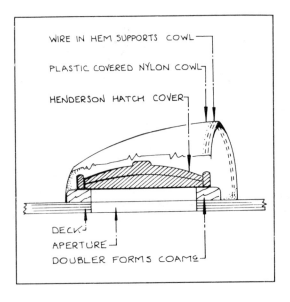

WIRE IN HEM SUPPORTS COWL

PLASTIC COVERED NYLON COWL

HENDERSON HATCH COVER

DECK
APERTURE
DOUBLER FORMS COAMG

Light, tight vent   To make this lightweight vent, a doubler is fitted on deck so that it stands up say 1 in. This forms the coaming, and a Henderson hatch cover fits on top. In bad weather the cover is clipped down to keep out water. At other times the cover is removed and the floppy soft vent, made from a plasticized cloth, scoops up the air. It can face forward or aft according to whether an extractor or inlet is wanted. To keep the vent standing open there is a length of stainless steel flexible wire in the seam. If anyone treads on the vent it collapses, but otherwise it stands up and directs the air flow. The cowl keeps out rain or spray and can be made to extend well beyond the hole through the deck in order to promote maximum air intake.

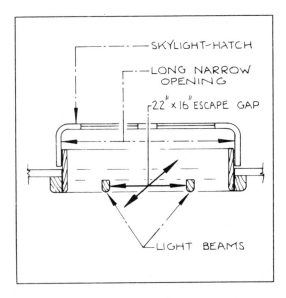

SKYLIGHT-HATCH

LONG NARROW OPENING

22" x 16" ESCAPE GAP

LIGHT BEAMS

Skylight stiffening   To make a cabin seem large, light and pleasant to live in, a big skylight is just the job. However a big aperture in the cabin top weakens the structure; even if the coachroof still easily withstands the weight of people walking about on it, a lot of flexing is likely and this results in leaks. However, there is no need for the beams in way of the skylight to be cut. They can span the open undecked gap, adding strength but taking away very little of the skylight's virtues. The beams are best set so that there is a gap big enough for a man to scramble through in an emergency, as this role of escape hatch is one of a skylight's side assets.

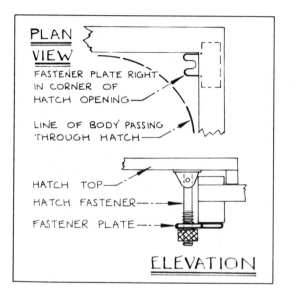

PLAN VIEW

FASTENER PLATE RIGHT
IN CORNER OF
HATCH OPENING —

LINE OF BODY PASSING
THROUGH HATCH —

HATCH TOP —
HATCH FASTENER —
FASTENER PLATE —

ELEVATION

No catch in the hatch　　A hatchway should be entirely free from obstructions, so that anyone can pass through in a hurry without getting a sweater or oilskins caught up or torn. However if the hatch is watertight and fitted with the type of securing device which is screwed down, the problem of keeping the opening clear is difficult.

The plates to take the screw-down type of fastener have open mouths and these are death to clothes or sails since they tear anything that catches on them. If they are set right in the corner of the hatchway there is a very good chance that they will do no damage, because they are virtually out of the line of anything passing through the opening. Ensure that the fasteners are held securely by screws or bolts as they take a heavy load when tightened down

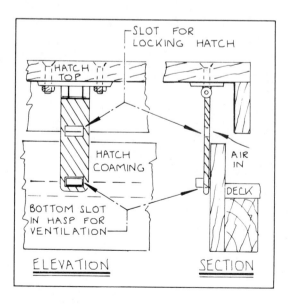

SLOT FOR
LOCKING HATCH

HATCH
TOP

HATCH
COAMING

AIR
IN

DECK

BOTTOM SLOT
IN HASP FOR
VENTILATION —

ELEVATION　　SECTION

Vent slot　　The forehatch hasp has two holes; when the hatch is shut the upper hole is used and the top of the hatch is then down tight. Normally a yacht can be left with the hasp raised so that the lower hole engages in the eye. The hatch top is then just high enough to let in a constant stream of air. It remains as burglar-proof as before, and rain or spray breaking over the bow cannot find its way below. In certain cases an existing hasp could be modified by making the extra aperture in it. The idea could also be used to allow cockpit seat locker tops to be left open a fraction for ventilation.

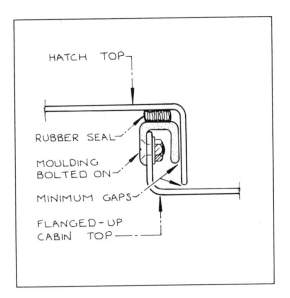

HATCH TOP

RUBBER SEAL

MOULDING
BOLTED ON

MINIMUM GAPS

FLANGED-UP
CABIN TOP

Hatch edge   Moulding fibreglass is simple enough within limitations. One thing which is very hard to achieve is a flange turned three or even two times in the same direction. Making an upstanding flange on a cabin top or deck is simple enough, but it tends to have a sharp upstanding edge which is unsightly and uncomfortable.

The upstanding flange can be covered by a channel which is bolted in place, the nuts being concealed. On the underside of the hatch top there is a strip or rubber glued all round to form a watertight seal. To help keep the water out there are two narrow gaps, between the flange and the hatch cover, and the hatch edge and the deck.

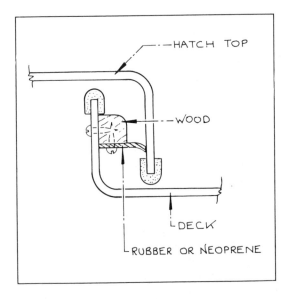

HATCH TOP

WOOD

DECK

RUBBER OR NEOPRENE

Additional hatch seal   Fix a wood rim round the upstanding flange of the deck. The corners of this rim must be carefully made to be watertight and the wood must be bedded on a good sealant or bedding compound. Fixing the thick ribbon of rubber or Neoprene can be difficult, and one way is to first make and fit the wood rim, then remove it and put on the rubber strip and finally refit the wood rim. The rubber strip should be just a little wider than the gap between the hatch flange and the deck flange so that it jams tight and keeps out water. The wood rim holding the rubber will also help to stop water flooding between the hatch coaming, if it extends close to the hatch top.

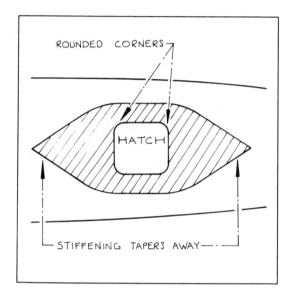

ROUNDED CORNERS

HATCH

STIFFENING TAPERS AWAY

Deck reinforcing   Boats built of a homogeneous material, such as fibreglass or welded steel, can be built lightly because they are not pierced by fastenings. For the strongest hull there should be no apertures at all; in practice owners insist on hatches, ports, cockpits, windows and other breaks in the continuous strength.

Where the shell is made as thin as possible there must be some strength compensation at each cut-out, in addition to well-rounded angles, otherwise cracks will commence due to stress concentration at the corners. This fact gives many problems to ship and aircraft designers, and now affects yachtsmen as lightweight fibreglass boats become more numerous. Hull or deck stiffening should extend fore and aft and taper away, to carry away the strains.

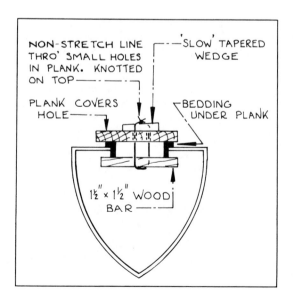

NON-STRETCH LINE THRO' SMALL HOLES IN PLANK. KNOTTED ON TOP

'SLOW' TAPERED WEDGE

PLANK COVERS HOLE

BEDDING UNDER PLANK

$1\frac{1}{2}'' \times 1\frac{1}{2}''$ WOOD BAR

Emergency hatch cover   When the top of a hatch came adrift on a small catamaran, the crew put together this jury rig. They laid strips of sticky, waterproof bedding tape (Sylglas) on the hatch coaming (shown black in the sketch) and lodged a strong wood bar under the coaming. This bar was held in place by a length of line, the ends of which were passed through holes in a piece of plank. The plank was put on the coamings and the two ends of the line tied together, leaving enough slack to slip in the nose of a wooden wedge. Hammering in the wedge tightened the temporary top down onto the coamings so effectively that no water got below even though waves washed over the decks regularly.

On a man-sized hatch two or even four lines and wedges may be called for and over a long period it may be necessary to tap them up tight every so often. The holes where the line passes through the top need sealing off with a waterproof stopper.

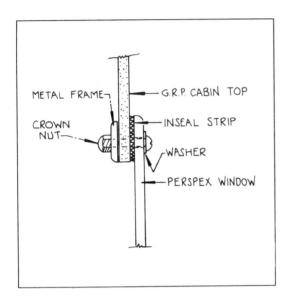

METAL FRAME

CROWN NUT

G.R.P. CABIN TOP

INSEAL STRIP

WASHER

PERSPEX WINDOW

Transparently simple   The type of window illustrated is perhaps a little primitive, but it has the advantage of being very lightweight and cheap. The round-head bolts should be spaced 2–3 in apart and the holes made for them should be one size too large, to prevent cracking in the window material (Perspex, Plexiglas or poly-carbonate). By using a proprietary sealing strip such as Inseal not only will the job be speeded up but also the appearance will be much neater than if a bedding compound from a tube is used. Any soft plasticy bedding never looks really smart regardless of the care used when applying it. The crown nuts have a limited depth and so the bolt lengths must be exactly right, if they are to be tight. Naturally all the corners of the aper-ture and the window material must be well rounded for both neatness and strength.

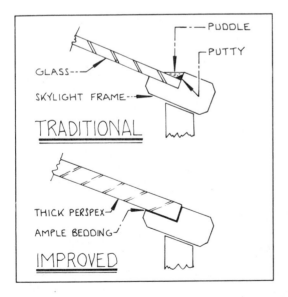

PUDDLE

PUTTY

GLASS

SKYLIGHT FRAME

TRADITIONAL

THICK PERSPEX

AMPLE BEDDING

IMPROVED

Leaking lights   The usual type of skylight glazing is relatively thin compared to the frame. Normally there is a recess along the bottom edge of each piece of glass where water can collect, and soon this puddle will find its way into the cabin, as well as rotting the frame. By using transparent, tough plastic there will be no increase in weight even though the material can be much thicker. If it stands slightly above the frame there is no chance of water lying in the join. Ample bedding material is used, and a flexible, non-hardening sealant such as Faro-caulk is ideal.

Perspex, Plexiglas or polycarbonate (Makrolon) may be used as replacements for glass. The latter is a new and extremely strong plastic material available in a variety of finishes and thicknesses, and offers protection against breakage or burglars.

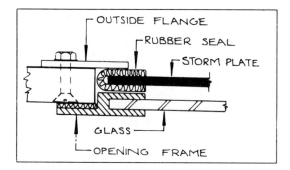

Stormproofing   Ports or windows anywhere on a boat are a source of weakness. Those in the topsides are particularly vulnerable and there should be some means of total closure in the event of the glass being cracked or broken. Many of the heavier type of ports have deadlights inside, but these are obtrusive and usually rather ugly. One manufacturer follows a completely different approach: he supplies his ports with portable storm plates which fit between the outside flange and the main window frame. It is true that the window frame has to be opened to fit the plates, and water could flood in while this is being done. However, many people always fit storm plates all round before leaving harbour if they are making a long passage. The idea can be adopted for many windows which have neither storm plates nor deadlights.

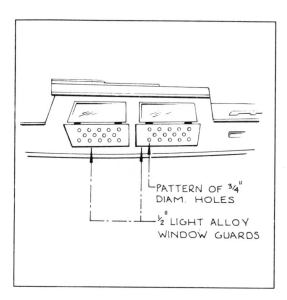

Window guards   A danger for any yacht, whether under sail or power, is that her windows will be broken in. Even in moderately heavy weather a big area of glass can be smashed in by a rogue sea caused by two waves superimposed to make an unusually high one.

A simple type of guard can be made from aluminium plate. Depending on the height of the windows above the deck, the guards are hinged in place, so that they can be swung up and secured by stiff turnbuttons when the sea rises. If space does not permit, they can be removed completely for stowing. To let in light and to give at least a restricted view out, there is a pattern of holes in each plate. The holes should be as small as possible and not closer than 4 in apart, while the hinges and turnbuttons should be massive.

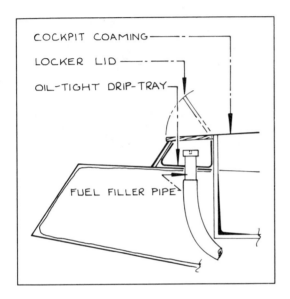

COCKPIT COAMING

LOCKER LID

OIL-TIGHT DRIP-TRAY

FUEL FILLER PIPE

Watertight filler   One source of engine
trouble is seawater in the fuel. It happens often
when the fuel filler pipe is flush with the deck,
because this type is hard to keep truly tight.

   It can be protected by a locker on the aft deck
between the aft and side cockpit coamings.
The raised screw top has a deep skirt extending
well down round the pipe with plenty of thread.
Round it is a drip tray so that spilt fuel does not
foul the deck; the special key for opening the
cap may be kept here. The same arrangement
may be used for the fresh water filler pipe,
since it needs comparable protection. Naturally
the water filler must be kept well away from the
fuel filler, and distinctively marked.

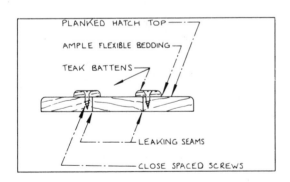

PLANKED HATCH TOP

AMPLE FLEXIBLE BEDDING

TEAK BATTENS

LEAKING SEAMS

CLOSE SPACED SCREWS

Leak beater   A hatch top which is made of
strips of wood with unglued seams between is
all too likely to leak. Teak battens (which also
form tread strips) can be screwed down over
each seam with lots of non-hardening bedding
compound such as Farocaulk. The screws are
close-spaced down only one side of the seam so
that when the wood comes and goes the seal
remains tight. The strips are set symmetrically to
give the whole job a neat appearance, but they
have to be measured from the outside edge of the
hatch top since they cannot be centred over the
seams if the screws are to be set neatly down the
middle of the battens. Tufnol might be used
instead of teak, possibly through-bolted instead
of screwed.

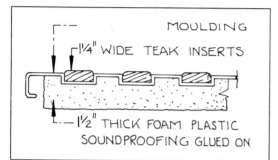

MOULDING

1¼" WIDE TEAK INSERTS

—1½" THICK FOAM PLASTIC SOUNDPROOFING GLUED ON

Cockpit sole panels   Fibreglass is a heavy and increasingly expensive material, so it should not be used in excessive quantity. At the same time cockpit soles need to be rigid. In one production 36-footer the sole is corrugated for stiffness and each corrugation has a fitted teak insert. Teak is easy to keep clean, moderately non-slip, gives a ship-shape appearance, and protects the fibreglass from abrasion.

A further advantage of this type of sole is that the overall weight is reasonable, always an asset for a panel that has to be lifted quite frequently. Soundproofing materials can be bought from specialist firms such as Revertex Ltd of London.

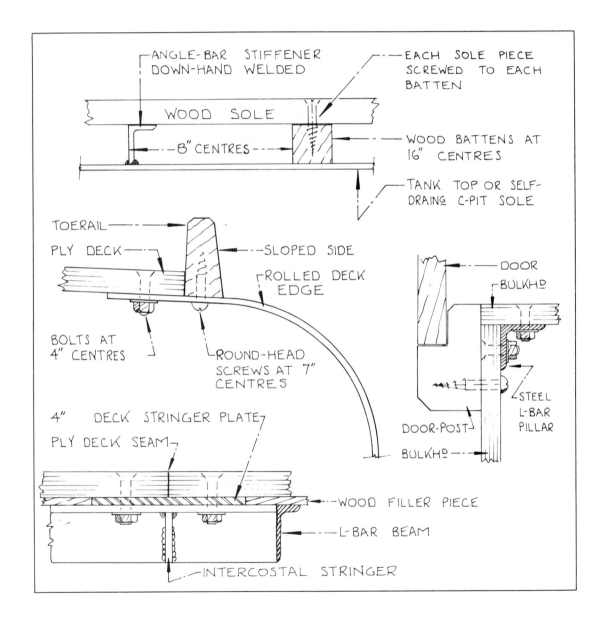

ANGLE-BAR STIFFENER
DOWN-HAND WELDED

EACH SOLE PIECE
SCREWED TO EACH
BATTEN

WOOD SOLE

8" CENTRES

WOOD BATTENS AT
16" CENTRES

TANK TOP OR SELF-
DRAING C-PIT SOLE

TOERAIL

PLY DECK

SLOPED SIDE

ROLLED DECK
EDGE

DOOR
BULKHD

BOLTS AT
4" CENTRES

ROUND-HEAD
SCREWS AT 7"
CENTRES

DOOR-POST

BULKHD

STEEL
L-BAR
PILLAR

4"   DECK STRINGER PLATE

PLY DECK SEAM

WOOD FILLER PIECE

L-BAR BEAM

INTERCOSTAL STRINGER

Steel yachts The top sketch shows how the cockpit sole of a 40 ft steel motor cruiser was made. The plate was laid down with one or two stiffeners welded across most of its width. After welding the plate to the shell, extra angle-bar stiffeners are put in at 16 in centres. The portable teak sole grating lies partly on the stiffeners and partly on special wood battens. As a result all welding is downhand and the relatively thin steel plate never buckles when anybody walks across it.

The middle sketch shows the deck edge rolled to give a smooth strong finish, with no edge for the paint to chip off. The main deck is of marine ply edged with a teak toerail. The latter is fastened from beneath so that no dowelling is needed and no fastenings show. Bottom left shows how the 4 ft wide marine ply deck panels are joined over a longitudinal stringer plate. If the deck becomes damaged it is a quick job to repair the affected panel.

The bottom right detail shows how a steel angle-bar carries two joining bulkheads. By welding the angle-bar to the frame, floor bar and beam, the deck is considerably stiffened. Notice how the doorpost shows no fastenings on the inside of the cabin as all the unsightly steel-work and fastenings are hidden.

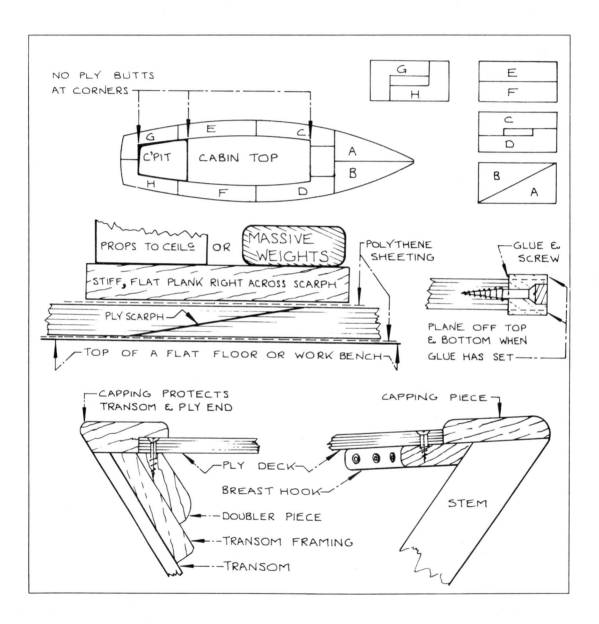

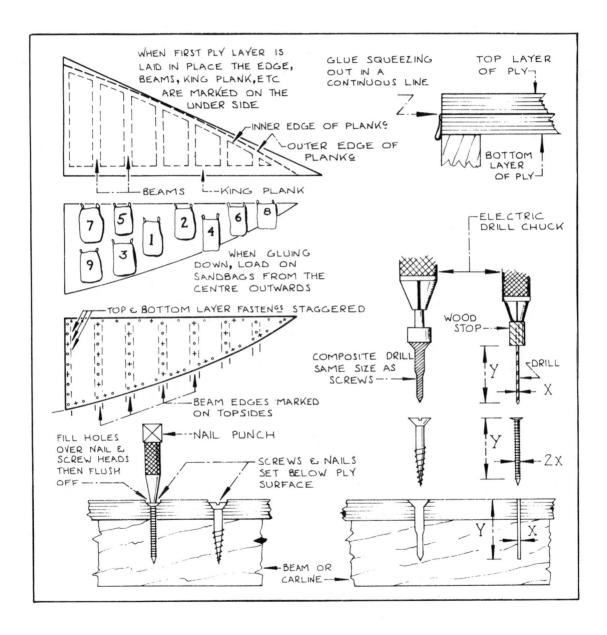

WHEN FIRST PLY LAYER IS LAID IN PLACE THE EDGE, BEAMS, KING PLANK, ETC ARE MARKED ON THE UNDER SIDE

INNER EDGE OF PLANKS

OUTER EDGE OF PLANKS

BEAMS — KING PLANK

GLUE SQUEEZING OUT IN A CONTINUOUS LINE

TOP LAYER OF PLY

BOTTOM LAYER OF PLY

WHEN GLUING DOWN, LOAD ON SANDBAGS FROM THE CENTRE OUTWARDS

TOP & BOTTOM LAYER FASTENGS STAGGERED

ELECTRIC DRILL CHUCK

WOOD STOP

COMPOSITE DRILL SAME SIZE AS SCREWS

DRILL

BEAM EDGES MARKED ON TOPSIDES

FILL HOLES OVER NAIL & SCREW HEADS THEN FLUSH OFF

NAIL PUNCH

SCREWS & NAILS SET BELOW PLY SURFACE

BEAM OR CARLINE

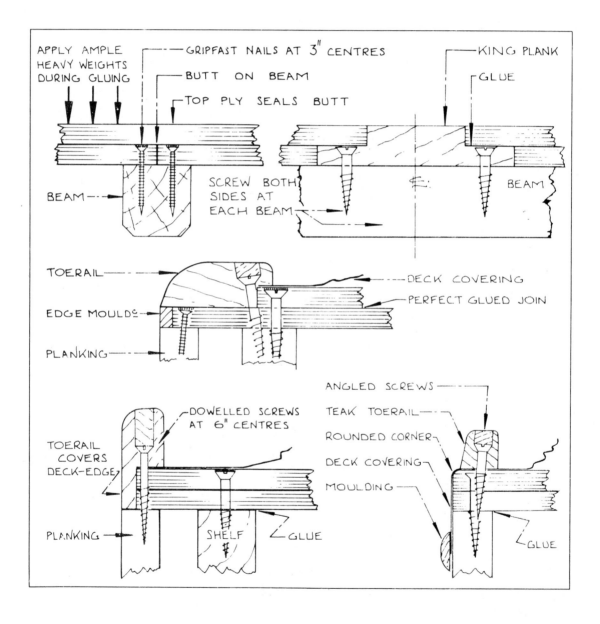

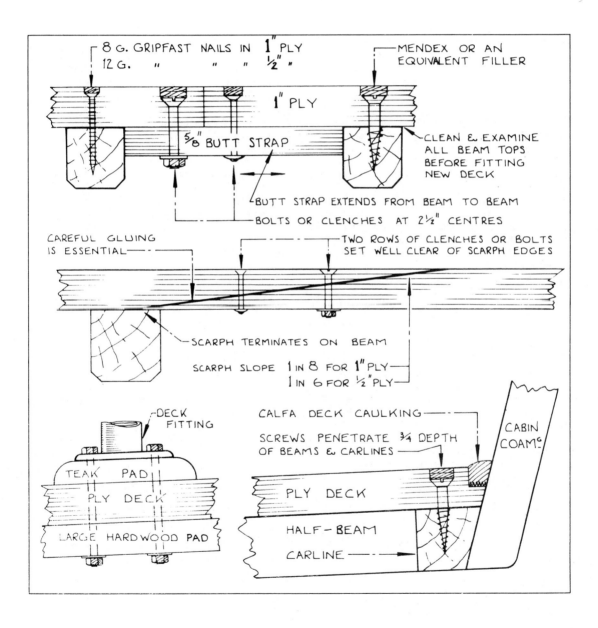

8 G. GRIPFAST NAILS IN 1" PLY
12 G.   "   "   " ½" "

MENDEX OR AN EQUIVALENT FILLER

1" PLY

⅝" BUTT STRAP

CLEAN & EXAMINE ALL BEAM TOPS BEFORE FITTING NEW DECK

BUTT STRAP EXTENDS FROM BEAM TO BEAM

BOLTS OR CLENCHES AT 2½" CENTRES

CAREFUL GLUING IS ESSENTIAL

TWO ROWS OF CLENCHES OR BOLTS SET WELL CLEAR OF SCARPH EDGES

SCARPH TERMINATES ON BEAM

SCARPH SLOPE 1 IN 8 FOR 1" PLY
1 IN 6 FOR ½" PLY

DECK FITTING

TEAK PAD
PLY DECK
LARGE HARDWOOD PAD

CALFA DECK CAULKING

SCREWS PENETRATE ¾ DEPTH OF BEAMS & CARLINES

CABIN COAM⁶

PLY DECK

HALF-BEAM

CARLINE

Redecking a wooden boat   So many troubles on wooden vessels start with the decks. Leaks cause common patterns of deterioration such as rotten beam ends, softening round the shelf fastenings, and so on. An otherwise useful and valuable boat will often by spoiled by a poor deck, yet renewal with plywood is not difficult.

Marine ply is the ideal material to use. It is sold in sheets 8 × 4 ft, but sometimes a number of 8 ft sheets are just too short to cover the full deck area. Some of the techniques described may help, along with careful pre-planning. As marine ply is costly it should be used carefully ; on no account should material which is below marine quality (BS 1088 or equivalents in other countries) be used. A scaled deck plan of the boat should be drawn. It must record the exact position of the deck fittings, and be measured from fixed points which will not be affected by the renewal of the decking. Apart from helping in the economical use of materials, it is not always possible to drill the bolt holes for deck fittings from below.

If a piece of ply is just a little too narrow to cover the side deck, glue and screw on a strip of solid wood to increase the width of the sheet. Make the strip too thick and when the glue has set hard plane off the surplus. Mark the positions of the screws on both faces of the sheet so that they will be missed when drilling for other fastenings.

When the ply is first put in place it should be positioned carefully but not fastened down. Go underneath and draw around all the structure to which the decking will be fastened, then take the ply off and turn it over. Drill through the ply down the centre between the marked lines so that the fastenings will go into the middle of the beams ; cut off any surplus round the deck edge. Turn it right way up for countersinking.

When the ply is in place for fastening it should be weighted extensively (sandbags are inexpensive) to hold it down and expel air. If two layers are being used take care to see that fastenings through the top piece do not foul those already in the lower one. As it is extremely hard to get two thicknesses to bond perfectly, ample glue must be used. One indication that enough has been used is the excess squeezed out along the edge. This should be continuous, and can be wiped off while soft.

To hold the ply decking down, the fastenings must be driven carefully in the correct size of hole. A few practice attempts in scrap wood are recommended ; time taken to set up correct drilling arrangements will be saved many times over during the real operation. Fastenings have to be sunk below the surface, and if a composite drill bit is used for screws then a countersink will almost certainly have to be used lightly afterwards, to ensure that the heads go down far enough. Once the fastenings are in, their heads are covered by stopping, which is allowed to harden and then cleaned off flush.

Where double layers of ply are used the butt join of the lower layer may be at a beam. The upper layer forms a wide butt strap and the beam supports the lower layer's edges until the top layer is joined on. A rebated king plank is a good way to make the centreline join. It avoids having the upper and lower fore-and-aft seams coinciding, and is a good way of gaining extra width where the ply is not quite wide enough to span the boat.

Various techniques can be used for finishing the deck edges. A wide toerail looks good on a styled motor cruiser, especially if the wood is deep and attractively varnished. However it does take up deck width and is not so good if the side decks are narrow. The toerail is sometimes set on the outside of the planking. This seldom looks smart, and damage from another vessel or a quay tends to cost twice as much as usual to repair. The toerail shown on the left is rather sophisticated and difficult to work, but it gives a very good finish. The simpler one that is set in slightly is quicker and cheaper to attach and may be more suitable where a sheet lead track is to be fitted on top. Teak is the ideal material for toe-rails, but mahogany is far cheaper, and easier to to buy. Softwoods are unsatisfactory since they do not stand the wear and tear.

Various forms of deck covering can be used, but canvas is now seldom seen because though it is cheap it does not last well. Cascover or glass cloth sheathing are expensive but give good service. Various cloths with plastic coatings, such as Trakmark, combine the low cost of canvas with the virtues of a longer lasting, non-skid surface.

Where the decking is a single layer of ply, a simple way of joining two adjacent pieces is shown in the fourth sketch. The butt strap extends from beam to beam and need not be quite as thick as the ply it joins. The ply can be fastened down to the beams with screws or ring nails; the latter are quicker to use and even when spaced closer are slightly lighter and cheaper. The butt strap fastenings can be clenched copper nails or bolts. Either way two people are needed to do the job, and clenching calls for a bit of practice.

Instead of a butt strap a scarph may be used, but the joint must be sufficiently long or it will be weak—six to eight times the thickness of the ply is about right. In theory the scarph needs no fastenings, but only practised shipwrights can work with nothing to pull the two sides together. Some people put in fastenings until the glue has set, then take them out and plug the holes.

Every deck fitting should have both a hardwood pad on the deck and another underneath. Ply edges should not be exposed so offcuts should only be used for underdeck pads.
Deck fittings must be bolted down, not screwed. There should be bedding compound under every pad and under the flange of the fitting; the fastenings should be of the same material as the fitting.

One way to finish off a ply deck edge against a cabin or hatch coaming is shown. Calfa caulking (sold by International Paints) is a flexible material which takes up expansion and contraction and replaces conventional caulking. This saves time and is convenient for anyone

unpractised in this art. The sketch also shows the depth to which screws should be driven to get a firm grip. The details of finishing off the ends of the boat may provide ways to overcome slight shortages of material.

As can be seen here, one of the advantages of a ply deck is that it forms a massive horizontal knee, making the whole boat more rigid.

Spars and Rigging

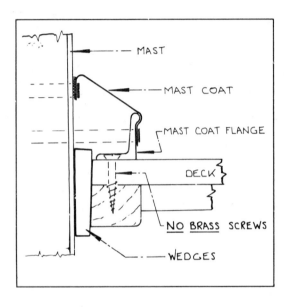

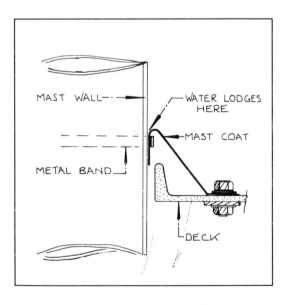

Mast coats   An aluminium mast through a wood deck is shown in the top drawing. To avoid electrolytic action there must be no cuprous fittings or fastenings round the mast. It might be thought that the screws holding the metal angle-bar could be of brass or bronze because they are inside the mast coat and should remain dry. But at sea the spray drives aboard hard, and everything is suffused with moisture, so that there is plenty of water and salt inside the mast coat. Once inside it cannot escape, so the mast is eaten away all the time and on occasions serious pitting occurs in the course of a few months.

One arrangement is to have the mast coat held to the spar by a big stainless steel hose clamp, with a flexible bedding material improving the seal. Another hose clamp encircles the metal angle-bar which extends right round the deck opening in a hoop, this bar being of aluminium alloy for preference.

An alternative technique is used on some GRP boats where the mast extends through the deck. Round the hole there is a moulded-in upstand, partly to deter water from going below but mainly to stiffen the deck. The coat is put on the mast, extending upwards. After it has been secured by its hose clamp the coat is turned over it and bolted to the deck at close intervals. The bolts embrace upper and lower metal rings which are bedded down with a flexible sealant and act as continuous washers.

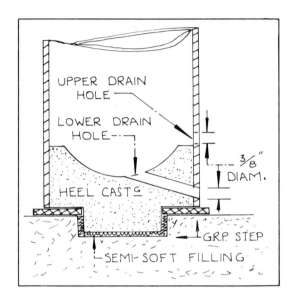

UPPER DRAIN
HOLE

LOWER DRAIN
HOLE

$\frac{3}{8}$" DIAM.

HEEL CAST͞G

G.R.P. STEP

SEMI-SOFT FILLING

Mast heel troubles   Corrosion is sometimes
seen around the heel casting of a metal mast,
and one way to check this is to keep the heel
dry. A hole drilled near the base of the mast
will let trapped water out, but it will probably be
necessary to have a second hole through both
the mast wall and the heel casting. Regardless of
the size of the mast these holes should be $\frac{3}{8}$ in
diameter or larger, otherwise they will get
blocked with dirt.

The socket which takes the heel tenon should
be filled with a semi-soft composition so that
there is no space left for the water to lie. Incidentally, it is bad practice for a mast to bear
directly down on fibreglass because this material
does not take kindly to high local loadings;
$\frac{1}{4}$ in ply could be used between the heel and
the fibreglass.

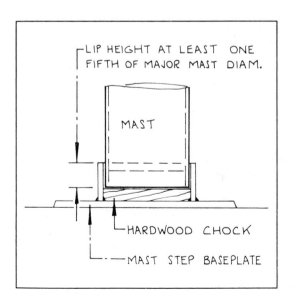

LIP HEIGHT AT LEAST ONE
FIFTH OF MAJOR MAST DIAM.

MAST

HARDWOOD CHOCK

MAST STEP BASEPLATE

Mast height adjustment   When stepping
a mast it is sometimes found that one of the
shrouds or stays is a fraction too long. It may
be possible to change the rigging screw for a
shorter pattern of equal strength, but a lighter
screw should never be used. The trick shown
here sometimes saves an embarrassing situation, though it only works when the mast
is stepped on deck in a cup with sturdy sides
which are of ample height. A piece of hardwood
is cut and dropped into the step; it should be
well painted or, if there is no time for this,
greased all over to exclude water. It is important not to raise the mast so that it has no
adequate 'fence' round the heel, sides about a
fifth of the major mast diameter in height being
considered safe in most conditions.

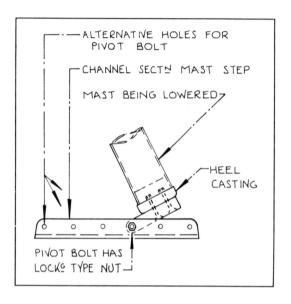

ALTERNATIVE HOLES FOR PIVOT BOLT

CHANNEL SECTⁿ MAST STEP

MAST BEING LOWERED

HEEL CASTING

PIVOT BOLT HAS LOCKᵍ TYPE NUT

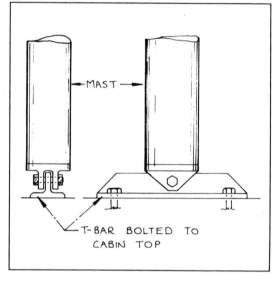

MAST

T-BAR BOLTED TO CABIN TOP

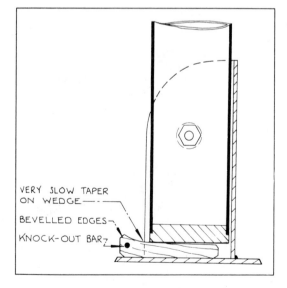

VERY SLOW TAPER ON WEDGE

BEVELLED EDGES

KNOCK-OUT BAR

Mast steps   Steel or aluminium channel bar makes a good base for a deck-stepped mast (top left). It spreads the load, gives alternate positions for the mast, and is cheap. Combined with the type of pivoting heel fitting shown (Ian Proctor Metal Masts Ltd) it is easy to step a small mast, and even a big one is made simpler to handle than usual.

A similar style of step may be made from inverted T-bar (top right), but the spar cannot be hinged up and a crane is needed for stepping. However, rake and fore-and-aft position are easy to adjust. Because so much load comes on a single bolt this arrangement is not recommended for boats over about 35 ft.

When a mast is stepped in a tabernacle, a stout wedge under the heel will transfer the mast compression load directly to the deck. The horizontal bolt (or bolts) through the spar are thus not asked to bear high stresses, which stops that worrying ovalizing in the mast and tabernacle in way of the bolts. The wedge must have a very slow taper indeed, and be of the hardest available wood. The knock-out bar should not be near the end or the grain will be split when tapping out the wedge.

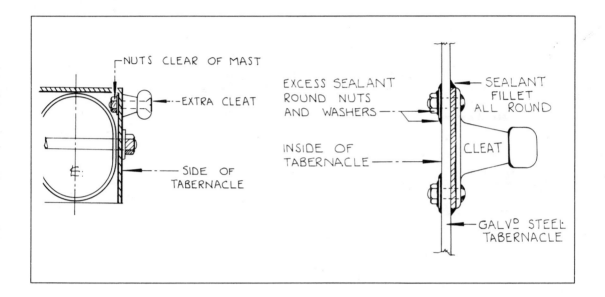

NUTS CLEAR OF MAST

EXTRA CLEAT

SIDE OF TABERNACLE

EXCESS SEALANT ROUND NUTS AND WASHERS

INSIDE OF TABERNACLE

SEALANT FILLET ALL ROUND

CLEAT

GALV? STEEL TABERNACLE

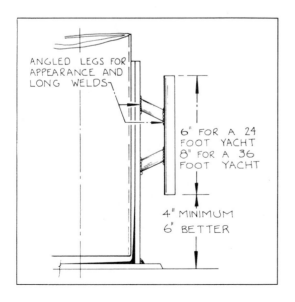

ANGLED LEGS FOR APPEARANCE AND LONG WELDS

6" FOR A 24 FOOT YACHT 8" FOR A 36 FOOT YACHT

4" MINIMUM 6" BETTER

Adding a cleat   It is not easy to add substantial cleats to an aluminium mast without special tools and fastenings and suitable fittings. However on a tabernacle ordinary bolts can be used, or the fitting welded on.

Even when the cleat and tabernacle appear to be of the same material, there is a good chance that the precise specification is different, and as there is likely to be electrolytic action between the two parts some form of insulation is needed. It may not be possible to fit sleeves around the bolts, but if liberal quantities of a flexible, non-hardening sealant (Farocaulk) are used there will be a fair measure of insulation and moisture exclusion. The sealant must be used inside the bolt holes and under washers, nuts and the fitting itself. Galvanized steel loses its protective coating where bolt holes have been drilled and such a seal is necessary for long life. A fillet of the bedding left around the joins and ledges will help to shed water so that it does not lie in tiny corroding puddles. When the sealant is still soft it should be partially wiped off to leave an even fillet.

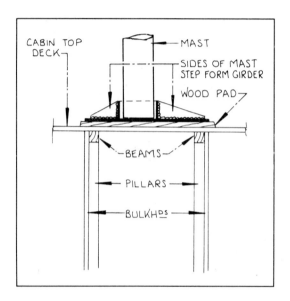

Structural mast step   Where a mast stands on the cabin top, the designer will sometimes want to avoid having a pillar immediately under it. A typical arrangement consists of two bulkheads each stiffened by a pair of deck beams forward and aft of the mast, possibly on either side of the toilet compartment or hanging locker. To spread the thrust of the mast between the supports there must be some structure extending fore and aft, logically the mast step. If the sides of the step are welded to the baseplate the result is a deep channel which has tremendous strength provided the sides are high and thick enough. The step is shown with tapered side plates to save weight and improve appearance; the maximum depth of side plate is only needed midway between the beams.

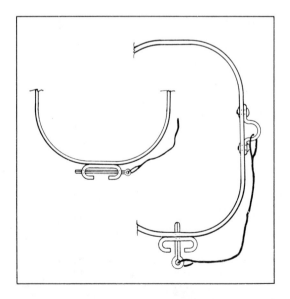

Track stop   Both of these stops will serve to keep the slides from dropping off the track when lowering sail. The split pin needs to be stainless steel for use on an aluminium mast, and needs a safety line which may be attached to a small riveted-on metal loop. The pin is a push fit in a hole drilled through the track and mast wall. If it can lie athwartships it will have a double bearing surface and be less likely to bend.

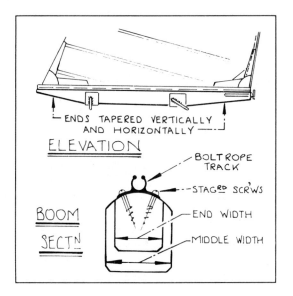

ENDS TAPERED VERTICALLY
AND HORIZONTALLY

ELEVATION

BOLT ROPE
TRACK

STAG͏ᴿᴰ SCR'WS

END WIDTH

MIDDLE WIDTH

BOOM
SECTᴺ

Wooden boom Now that so many yachts use aluminium spars it is easy to forget the advantages of a wood boom. Wood may be cheaper, particularly where some special feature is required. For instance, when the minimum section of boom is needed it is easier to taper a wooden spar than an aluminium one. This is an advantage where the mainsheet is not at the extreme outer end. If a bendy boom is required, a wooden one can be made extra thick and planed away gradually until it has just the right degree of bend.

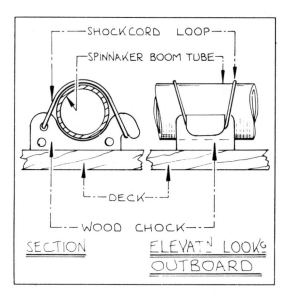

SHOCKCORD LOOP

SPINNAKER BOOM TUBE

DECK

WOOD CHOCK

SECTION

ELEVATᴺ LOOKᴳ
OUTBOARD

Securing the pole Spinnaker boom chocks are easily made from hardwood. If the boom is wood the chocks should have their top surfaces padded to prevent the booms from being damaged as they are dropped in place by crews in a whirl of hurry. As the spar is raised slightly off the deck, dirt and water cannot lodge underneath.

Each chock needs at least four large screws to hold it down, and these must be driven upwards. For a yacht over about 28 ft bolts through the chocks and deck would be better. A fibreglass deck could have the chocks incorporated in the moulding, and they could even form part of the deck stiffening.

When not racing, or when the foredeck is taking water, non-stretch lashings are necessary; they can be passed through the small holes shown. Shockcord is not adequate.

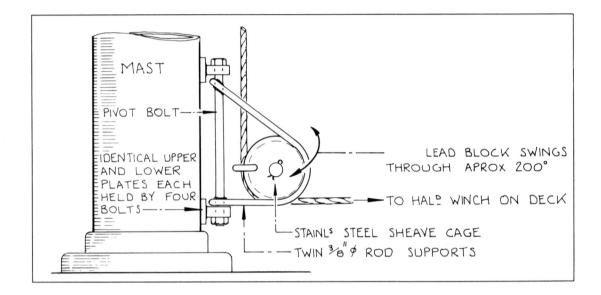

MAST

PIVOT BOLT- - -◄

IDENTICAL UPPER
AND LOWER
PLATES EACH
HELD BY FOUR
BOLTS - - -◄

LEAD BLOCK SWINGS
THROUGH APROX 200°

TO HAL⁰ WINCH ON DECK

—STAINLˢ STEEL SHEAVE CAGE
—TWIN ⅜" ⌀ ROD SUPPORTS

Pivoting lead block If a winch breaks down
the halyard can conveniently be led via the
block to any other winch, over an arc of about
200°. Also, if the halyard is hoisted by hand it
doesn't matter where the crew on the tail is
standing. For hoisting someone up the mast, the
tail can even be lead to the anchor winch.

The sheave can easily be removed for servicing
or renewing by undoing the split pin, and the
two eyeplates on the mast are standardized to
keep down production costs.

THREE STAINLS STEEL BAR CLEATS

STAINLS STEEL PEDESTAL

HALD WINCHES P.&.S. ANGLED TO SHEAVES

MAIN & JIB HALDS

VARIABLE POSITION MAST STEP

A clean mast foot This is an interesting internal halyard arrangement The foot of the mast is uncluttered by winches or cleats, which are grouped well back from the mast on a quadrilateral pedestal of stainless steel. The winches for the main and jib halyards are set at just the right angle to take the ropes emerging from the mast base. Both winches are low down so that their handles do not rotate much over 180°. It is easy enough to hoist the sails most of the way by hand; only the final tightening needs the added beef of a winch. Instead of conventional cleats there are horizontal bars of matching stainless steel welded across the winch base and extending beyond it. The mast step is elongated with a row of holes so that the mast can be moved to improve helm balance.

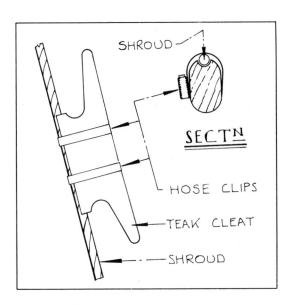

SHROUD

SECT<u>N</u>

HOSE CLIPS

TEAK CLEAT

SHROUD

Circus cleat An extra cleat can be difficult to secure on a boat with a fibreglass hull and an aluminium mast. One alternative is to fit the cleat to a shroud by cutting a groove along the base of the cleat. The traditional method of holding such a cleat in place was with seizings, but the quick, tough modern method is by using a pair of hose clips. There must be at least two of these clips, and as the galvanized type tend to rust rather quickly this is a good place to use stainless steel, especially on stainless rigging wire. The name of this cleat comes from the fact that it balances on a wire like a trapeze artist. For neatness the clips are recessed into the wood, and all edges are bevelled or rounded.

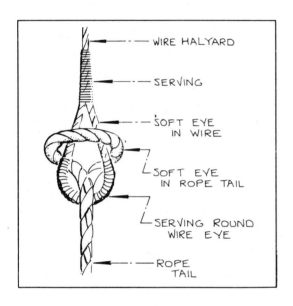

WIRE HALYARD

SERVING

SOFT EYE
IN WIRE

SOFT EYE
IN ROPE TAIL

SERVING ROUND
WIRE EYE

ROPE
TAIL

Halyard join   Joining a wire halyard to its rope tail can be a bit of a problem for anybody who is not able to do a wire-to-rope splice. The join shown is unconventional but has much to commend it. It is light and simple, and the rope can easily be renewed—or the wire changed—without throwing away the other part. A soft eye with a fairly big loop is made in the wire, say 3 in long for a 30 footer. The bottom of the loop is served so that there is reasonable cushioning. The rope tail is then spliced as a long soft eye and the two eyes are joined by passing one through the other. This join is compact and will pass round a big winch barrel, though not over a normal sheave.

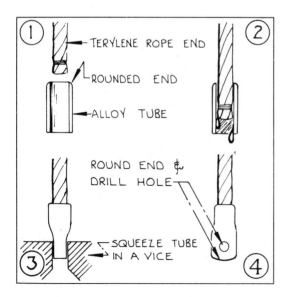

① TERYLENE ROPE END

ROUNDED END

ALLOY TUBE

②

ROUND END &
DRILL HOLE

③ SQUEEZE TUBE
IN A VICE

④

Rope ends   This method of finishing off a rope's end was invented by a Canadian catamaran enthusiast. He uses short lengths of aluminium tube which fit neatly over the bitter ends of the halyards. Before fitting the tube he rounds the end (1), then applies an epoxy cement such as Araldite to the end of the tube and slides the rope in (2). Next he clamps the aluminium tube to flatten the extreme end (3). After the resin has cured a hole is drilled through the flattened end so that it can be shackled to the foot of the mast to prevent the halyard going aloft by accident.

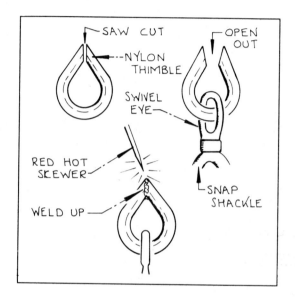

Modern hard eye   Except for very hard use, it is now common practice to use nylon thimbles to form hard eyes in rope. These thimbles are moulded without joins, unlike metal eyes which are bent round and can be forced open at the sharp end to take a closed ring or eye. With a nylon thimble a hacksaw is used to make a cut at the sharp end. It is easy to spring the gap open and then seal it with a red-hot skewer. The softened nylon should be stroked gently over the saw cut on both sides to lock the ends together.

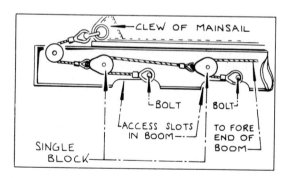

Clew tackle   On yachts up to about 30 ft overall a 4 : 1 purchase is often ample on the mainsail outhaul. This can be achieved using two single blocks as detailed in this sketch ; such blocks are small and will fit inside an aluminium boom. This makes a tidy tackle with nothing hanging down even when the gear is slack.

The outhaul shown is best used when the mainsheet is not on the end of the boom, since the access slots in the boom weaken it slightly. However, unless the slots are very large, they should not make much difference to a typical cruiser boom because they are so near the end. The fall of the tackle comes out through a slot at the fore end of the boom.

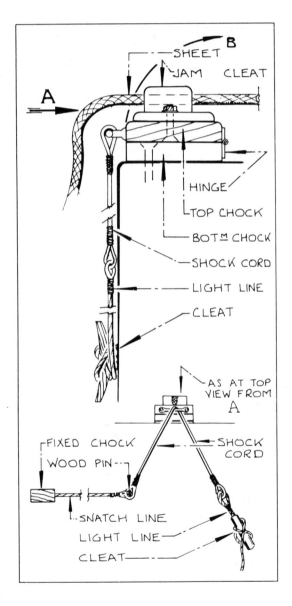

Sheet release   A simple reliable sheet release device is an advantage on catamarans and trimarans, and the one detailed here is easy to make and adjust. The top sketch is a side view with the sheet leading to the sail, away to the right. The sheet is held in a jam cleat bolted to a hardwood chock ; this is joined to a second identical chock by a strong bronze hinge, care being taken that the hinge has a bronze hinge, care being taken that the hinge has a bronze pin otherwise it will rust and sieze. Opposite the hinge there is a strongly fastened eye and a length of shockcord which can have its tension varied by pulling down on the light line fastened to the cleat at the bottom. A sudden squall puts an extra strain on the sheet which pulls the jam cleat up and over (B).

Below, an alternative layout is shown. The shockcord is passed through the eye on the upper chock and its end slipped over a headless wooden pin. Also on this pin is a snatch line which has its other end secured to a chock. Anyone seeing a squall coming simply grabs the snatch line and pulls it towards himself. This throws the shockcord off the wooden pin and releases the sheet. The snatch line can be extended to left and right, or up and down, so as to be operable from any position in the cockpit or even from the cabin.

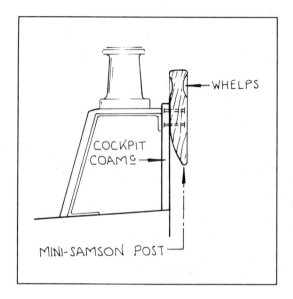

WHELPS

COCKPIT
COAMᵍ

MINI-SAMSON POST

Sheet cleat   This attractive and unusual anchorage for jib and genoa sheets is a miniature samson post bolted to the cockpit coaming. Bronze whelps at the top of the post take the wear, and the bottom is faired to a point so that the rope jams between the cleat and the coaming. Working space is left between it and the winch; a gap of about 8 in is probably about right for a 30 ft yacht.

Dimensions depend on circumstances and vary with the size of yacht, sail area, etc. For a 30 ft yacht a vertical height of 6–9 in should be right; the section should be about $1\frac{1}{2} \times 1\frac{1}{2}$ in and 3×3 in.

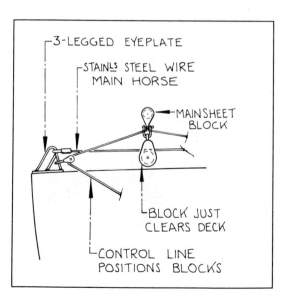

3-LEGGED EYEPLATE

STAINLˢ STEEL WIRE
MAIN HORSE

MAINSHEET
BLOCK

BLOCK JUST
CLEARS DECK

CONTROL LINE
POSITIONS BLOCKS

Light, cheap mainsheet horse   For craft of Quarter Ton size this type of horse has its advantages. It does not require a strong beam right across, only strong points at each end; it is cheaper than the normal X-section track with its roller carriage and is easier to remove and reposition when rerigging.

The three-legged eyeplate also doubles as a securing point for items like spinnaker lead blocks, lifelines, fenders etc. An ordinary eyeplate can be used but it will probably need chocking up off the deck. The control lines for hauling the mainsheet across are likely to need some form of tackle, or they can be led to a winch.

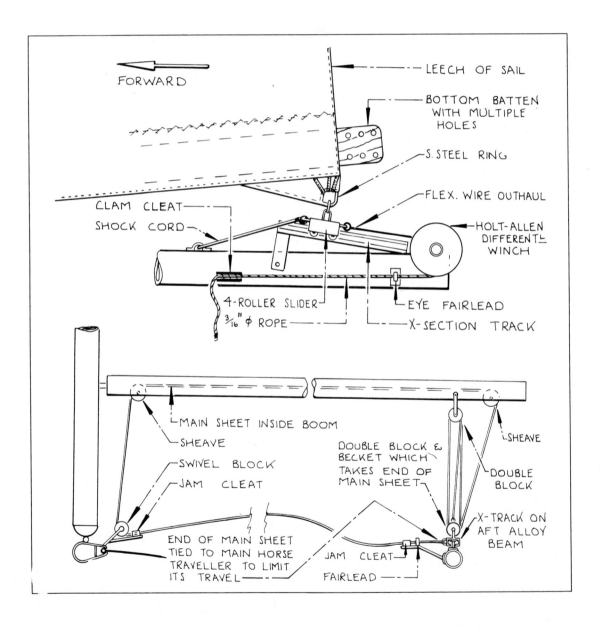

FORWARD

LEECH OF SAIL

BOTTOM BATTEN
WITH MULTIPLE
HOLES

S. STEEL RING

FLEX. WIRE OUTHAUL

CLAM CLEAT

SHOCK CORD

HOLT-ALLEN
DIFFERENTL
WINCH

4-ROLLER SLIDER

3/16" ø ROPE

EYE FAIRLEAD

X-SECTION TRACK

MAIN SHEET INSIDE BOOM

SHEAVE

SWIVEL BLOCK

JAM CLEAT

DOUBLE BLOCK &
BECKET WHICH
TAKES END OF
MAIN SHEET

SHEAVE

DOUBLE
BLOCK

END OF MAIN SHEET
TIED TO MAIN HORSE
TRAVELLER TO LIMIT
ITS TRAVEL

JAM CLEAT

FAIRLEAD

X-TRACK ON
AFT ALLOY
BEAM

Sophisticated sail controls Angling a
length of X-section track down towards the aft
end of the boom ensures that as the clew is
hauled aft the tension on the leech is increased
and the sail flattened. To give the necessary
power there is a standard differential winch; wire
round the axle runs to the traveller on the track.
To flatten the sail foot the helmsman merely
grabs the differential winch line and jolts it
forward, then resecures it in the Clam cleat on
the boom.

The boom is shown below, with the mainsheet
passing through it. To haul in the boom the
mainsheet is pulled from the foot of the mast
where there is a jam cleat to hold it.

The tail of the mainsheet limits the travel of
the mainsheet slider so the helmsman only has
to hold one piece of rope for two jobs. There are
no loose rope ends to go overboard since the
tackle end of the mainsheet is made fast to the
lower block. Having the mainsheet inside the
boom prevents it from sagging and decapitating
the helmsman. On a fast-moving boat like a
B-Class cat it is bad practice to look aft for any
reason, which makes it doubly sensible to have
the mainsheet coming to the hand from forward.

Deck Gear

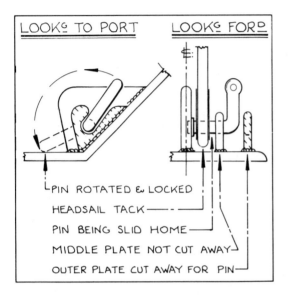

LOOK<u>S</u> TO PORT   LOOK<u>S</u> FOR<u>D</u>

⌐PIN ROTATED & LOCKED

HEADSAIL TACK———

PIN BEING SLID HOME——

MIDDLE PLATE NOT CUT AWAY⌐

OUTER PLATE CUT AWAY FOR PIN⌐

Tack pin   On the stemhead fitting of the Nicholson 43 there is a stainless steel fitting for securing the headsail tack. It is duplicated port and starboard and consists of five vertical plates with two locking bars. Each bar, which is simply a stainless rod bent at right angles with a safety line eye on the handle end, can be rotated and slid outboard. To open the tack hole, the end is lifted off the deck and turned forward. This allows it to be pulled outboard, as the handle can then slide past the outboard plate. Until the handle is right forward the outboard plate acts as a stop. The bar cannot come right out as there is a welded washer on its inner end which cannot pass through the hole on the middle plate. The sketch shows the bar after it has been pushed in to engage the tack, but before being pulled aft to lock.

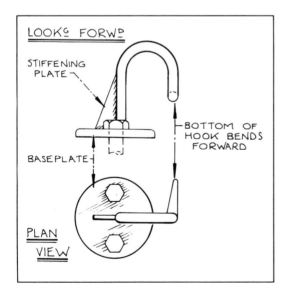

LOOK<u>S</u> FORW<u>D</u>

STIFFENING PLATE⌐

BASEPLATE⌐

—BOTTOM OF HOOK BENDS FORWARD

<u>PLAN</u>
<u>VIEW</u>

A pig's tail   This fitting is to take the headsail tacks, but it can be used in other locations, such as temporary forward holdfasts for the spinnaker sheets when they are not in use. In modern boats racing hard, the diameter of the hook and its fastenings will have to be large to withstand the high loadings on halyards and luff wires.

   The 'tail' has no moving parts, just a curl over the top and a bend forward at the tip. The tack thimble is engaged before the hanks are clipped on, and by virtue of the double bend the tack will stay in place. Very occasionally it might come off when the sail is lowered, if by a thousand-to-one chance the sail falls in a certain way.

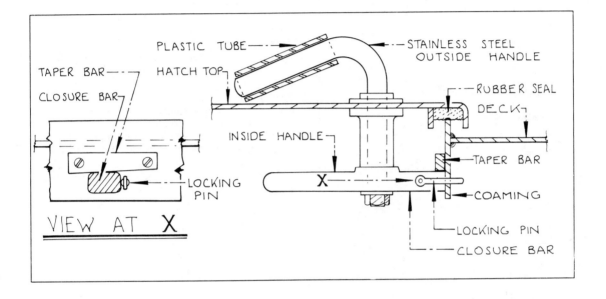

PLASTIC TUBE — STAINLESS STEEL OUTSIDE HANDLE

TAPER BAR — HATCH TOP

CLOSURE BAR — RUBBER SEAL — DECK

INSIDE HANDLE — TAPER BAR

X — COAMING

LOCKING PIN — LOCKING PIN

CLOSURE BAR

VIEW AT X

Metal hatch lock   On this aluminium 59 ft
Luders yawl the forehatch can be closed from
inside or on deck, and locked from inside. A
stainless steel handle has a shank which passes
through the metal hatch. The outer part is bent
over to minimize the risk of lines catching on it
and is insulated with thick plastic tube. There are
two of these handles, each of which can be
locked from inside by a pin which passes into a
hole in the internal coaming. The closure bar
engages under a tapered bar on the coaming,
forcing the hatch down tight and compressing
the rubber seal. No water can get in even
though the hatch stands only an inch or so above
the deck. The handle, taper bar and locking
pin are steel; the rest aluminium in this case,
though the design would also suit a steel deck
and hatch.

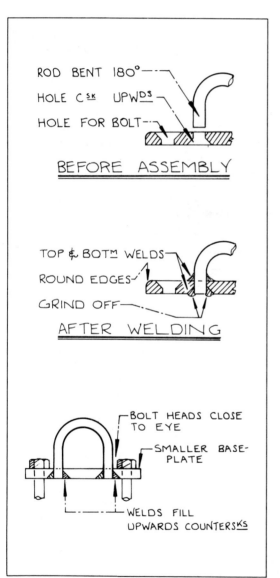

ROD BENT 180° ---

HOLE C^{sk} UPW^{DS} ---

HOLE FOR BOLT---

BEFORE ASSEMBLY

TOP & BOT^{M} WELDS---

ROUND EDGES---

GRIND OFF---

AFTER WELDING

BOLT HEADS CLOSE TO EYE

SMALLER BASE-PLATE

WELDS FILL UPWARDS COUNTERSK^{KS}

Eyeplate   An eyebolt should be used only for light loads ; an eyeplate with its two or more fastenings and a baseplate spreading the load is stronger. Plates are forged or fabricated, but castings should not be trusted.

Eyeplates can be made by first making the baseplate with countersunk holes for the ends of the bent rod. The rod drops through the holes and the ends are welded top and bottom, then ground off. Alternatively the weld may be only on the underside of the plate, for a neater finish. This allows the bolt heads to be closer to the eye if desired, giving a slightly smaller baseplate and lighter fitting.

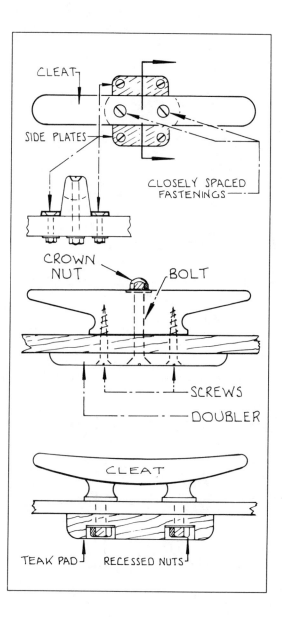

CLEAT

SIDE PLATES

CLOSELY SPACED
FASTENINGS

CROWN
NUT

BOLT

SCREWS

DOUBLER

CLEAT

TEAK PAD

RECESSED NUTS

Cleats In theory every cleat is rock-solid, immovable, and able to take twenty times its expected load. In practice they often become loose and are hard to resecure rigidly. The first step is to tighten the fastenings after applying glue where possible. By way of added bracing a pair of metal or hard plastic side plates will hold a cleat against rotational movement. This is more of a palliative than a guaranteed cure, and the plates must be fitted hard up against the cleat base (top).

Cleats should be long enough to have two or even three bolts through them, and when they are the trouble occurs less often. If there is scarcely room for two bolts, a single one and two chunky screws are almost as effective. The doubler is always important, and the crown nut is vastly to be preferred to a common nut which gives an unfinished look. The bolt, being countersunk, matches the screws in the pad in appearance.

If a cleat is secured to the deck its bolts will protrude into the cabin. A recessed internal pad does not reduce the available headroom and means that no one gets a nasty scalping from the nuts. The pad both spreads the load and improves appearance without making it necessary to tighten the nuts every other season (bottom).

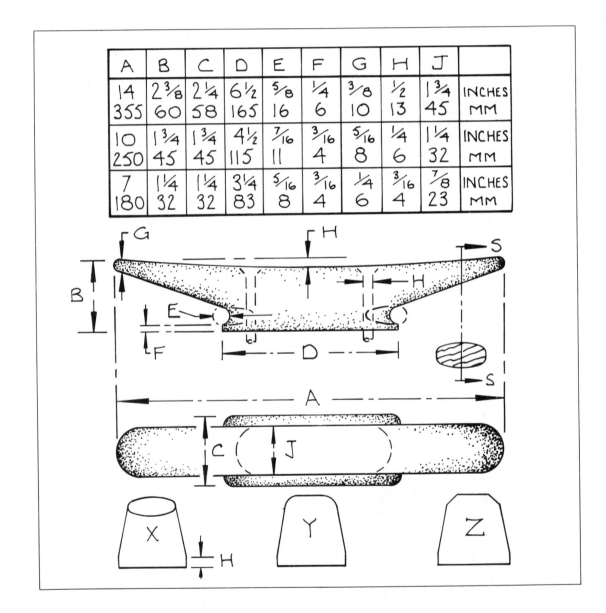

A	B	C	D	E	F	G	H	J	
14	$2\frac{3}{8}$	$2\frac{1}{4}$	$6\frac{1}{2}$	$\frac{5}{8}$	$\frac{1}{4}$	$\frac{3}{8}$	$\frac{1}{2}$	$1\frac{3}{4}$	INCHES
355	60	58	165	16	6	10	13	45	MM
10	$1\frac{3}{4}$	$1\frac{3}{4}$	$4\frac{1}{2}$	$\frac{7}{16}$	$\frac{3}{16}$	$\frac{5}{16}$	$\frac{1}{4}$	$1\frac{1}{4}$	INCHES
250	45	45	115	11	4	8	6	32	MM
7	$1\frac{1}{4}$	$1\frac{1}{4}$	$3\frac{1}{4}$	$\frac{5}{16}$	$\frac{3}{16}$	$\frac{1}{4}$	$\frac{3}{16}$	$\frac{7}{8}$	INCHES
180	32	32	83	8	4	6	4	23	MM

Rugged cleats   A cleat should be almost
unbreakable and at least 40 per cent bigger than
those fitted on most standard boats, and for
every two cleats there should be a spare. The
proportions shown, for three different sizes of
cleats, have been worked out from experience to
give strength, simple fabrication, easy use, and
good appearance. Hollowing the ridge (dimension
H) is important for good looks, and even more
important is the sloping in of the sides. The best
section is shown bottom left (X) ; a simpler
version has a flat top (Y), and an even simpler
one has bevelled edges at the top (Z). On no
account should the sides be left parallel : this
results in a shape which looks primitive and is
less convenient to use. All edges should be
rounded ; in particular the throat where ropes
lodge should be extremely well faired with a
round rasp or Surform. In the plan view the
broken line shows how the throat should be
rounded.

   Teak is the best wood for cleats, but failing this
many of the reliable hardwoods are a reasonable
substitute. The harder the wood the better,
since there is inevitably a lot of chafe. Bolts
rather than screws should be used, and in the
largest size a good case can be made for using
three of them. When making a cleat the outline
should first be marked out on the side of the
piece of wood and then the two holes drilled
(of diameter E). Saw cuts are made to meet these
holes, starting up from the base and then
slanting down from the ends of the horns.
Tapering the sides should be left as late as
possible because once this is done the cleat is
more difficult to hold in a vice. The taper should
not be carried right down to the base ; a small
flat is left all round, shown as dimension H on
section X.

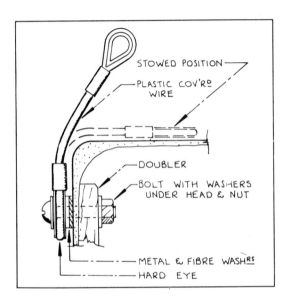

STOWED POSITION

PLASTIC COV'R\u1d30 WIRE

DOUBLER

BOLT WITH WASHERS UNDER HEAD & NUT

METAL & FIBRE WASH\u1d3fS

HARD EYE

Take-off point   On every sort of craft there is a need for strong points. They may be required to take sheet lead blocks, the steadying sail sheet blocks on a little motor cruiser, the lashings for a dinghy on deck, or the ends of lifelines. There are plenty of methods for spreading point loads on delicate hulls, but this one sometimes comes in useful where others cannot conveniently be used. The bolt must be of ample size, but the doubler is also vital. This design is not suitable for loads over about 500 lbs, and assumes the fibreglass is sufficiently thick. With some wood or metal hulls, and with adequate components, greater strains can be taken. But once the load reaches the order of a third of a ton, an eyeplate with two or four bolts is essential to take the load.

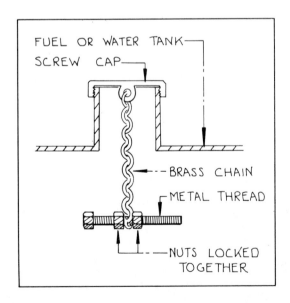

FUEL OR WATER TANK

SCREW CAP

BRASS CHAIN

METAL THREAD

NUTS LOCKED TOGETHER

Cap catcher   There is nothing worse than losing the cap off a fuel or water tank, for any temporary substitute is liable to let in rain or seawater. In this simple method of securing the fuel tank filler cap the metal thread shown is a brass bolt of about $\frac{1}{4}$ in diameter threaded right up to the head. Two nuts on it are tightened against each other so that they lock firmly at the point of balance. The chain is just long enough to allow the cap to be unscrewed and laid on the deck close to the filler. Brass lavatory chain is quite strong enough for the job.

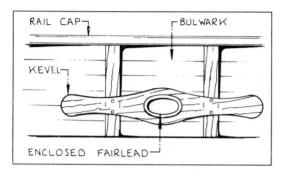

Kevel   Mooring kevels are seen on some recently built craft, both for their practicality and to maintain the theme of rugged, go-anywhere boats which can take a hammering at sea or in harbour. The kevel is nothing more than a gigantic cleat extending beyond two frames and bolted on. This version is swollen out in the middle and cut away with an oval aperture right through the bulwark; the hole is lined with a softly rounded metal fairlead so that warps can be led through. Closed fairleads are the only kind to use when there is a big rise and fall of tide which might lift a warp out of an open lead, and are ideal for any craft likely to be left unattended.

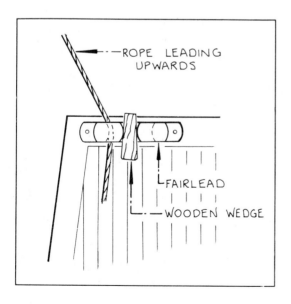

Open fairleads   If a line is lead from a fairlead up to a quay wall there is a good chance that it will pull out. Even if the vessel is attended she will range about until the line can be thrust back into the fairlead by the crew, who may be asleep when it comes free. All that is needed is a wooden wedge, driven in once the rope is in place. The wedge should have a slow taper and be hammered well into the fairlead mouth so that the metal arms bite into the wood. This trick is particularly useful if a boat has to be left for a prolonged period.

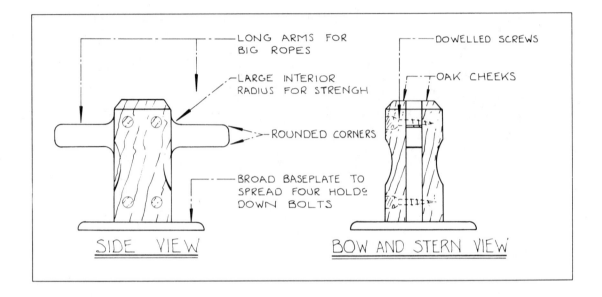

LONG ARMS FOR BIG ROPES

LARGE INTERIOR RADIUS FOR STRENGH

ROUNDED CORNERS

BROAD BASEPLATE TO SPREAD FOUR HOLD? DOWN BOLTS

DOWELLED SCREWS

OAK CHEEKS

SIDE VIEW

BOW AND STERN VIEW

Samson post   A mooring post and towing bollards can be made to the same sensible pattern. The basic fitting is of galvanized steel with a baseplate large enough to spread the four holding-down bolts and distribute the stress over a large area of deck. The upright post stands high enough to take chunky warps. The steel is rounded at the corners so that the galvanizing is less easily chipped off, and for appearance. Hard oak cheeks protect the ropes and are replaceable.

   For an 18–22 ft workboat a post about 8 in high and 3×3 in in section makes sense. The baseplate should be about 8 in square and $\frac{1}{4}$ in thick, with the vertical centre plate $\frac{3}{8} - \frac{1}{2}$ in thick. The arms ought to protrude at the very least 3 in on each side, and 4 in is better. Larger craft require more rugged dimensions.

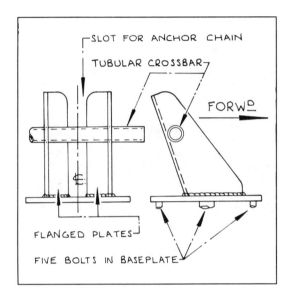

SLOT FOR ANCHOR CHAIN

TUBULAR CROSSBAR

FORWᴰ

FLANGED PLATES

FIVE BOLTS IN BASEPLATE

Metal mooring bitts   This fitting is a simple steel assembly which functions as both mooring bitts and chain stopper. It has a central slot into which the chain can be dropped, and this is particularly convenient when getting up the anchor singlehanded. Standing aft of the bitts and hauling on the chain, it will be found that each link rides easily over the sloped back of the flanged plates. When the chain is slacked off the links drop between the two back plates and the chain is held in place. The tubular crossbar stops the chain dropping down too far and is also used for turning the chain up on when riding to moorings. The baseplate is secured to the deck by one large and four small bolts, and anyone making the fitting should take care over the welding.

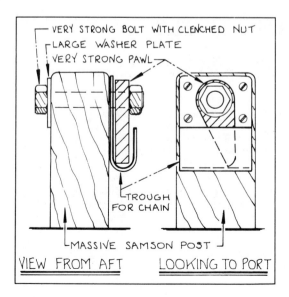

VERY STRONG BOLT WITH CLENCHED NUT
LARGE WASHER PLATE
VERY STRONG PAWL

TROUGH FOR CHAIN

MASSIVE SAMSON POST

VIEW FROM AFT   LOOKING TO PORT

Poor man's anchor winch   Each time a wave passes, the anchor chain slackens and tightens as the yacht plunges up and down. On the downward surge of the bow the load on the chain is quite small, so that it is not too hard to get in some cable without a winch. However the slack period lasts only a few seconds before the massive strain comes back, doubly heavy because the bow is soaring up.

By leading the anchor chain through a short, stout trough which has a pawl in it, the crew can snatch in the chain when it slackens, then rest while it comes tight. A very skilled crew can do this without the pawl, as they can snatch a turn round the samson post. But this is very tricky, and slower since they cannot haul in as every wave passes.

The pawl is sometimes seen on the stemhead fitting.

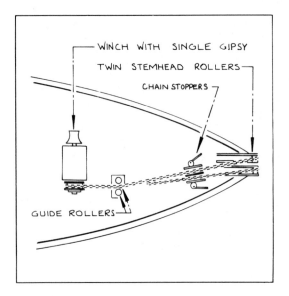

Two into one will go   When a yacht needs two anchors she also normally needs a winch with two gypsies, but if a boat has a single-gypsy windlass the owner may hesitate to buy an entirely new winch. Not many windlasses can be converted, and there is always the difficulty of lining up the second gypsy with its stem-head roller.

All that is needed is a pair of vertical rollers. They must be set just in front of the gypsy, to lead whichever chain is being hauled home in the precise line to feed correctly onto the windlass. Unless the chain is under $\frac{5}{16}$ in a pair of chain stoppers will be needed to hold the chains while one is taken off the winch to put the other on.

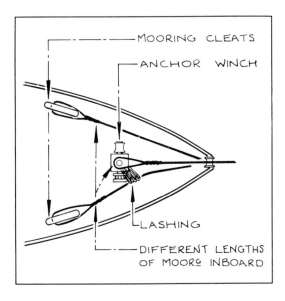

Fatigue fractures   Quite a few yachts moor up on a wire strop which leads from the permanent mooring chain to the securing point on deck. This technique is especially popular where the water is deep, in Scottish lochs for instance. However, a weakness of the arrangement is that the wire fatigues where it passes over the stemhead roller. The trouble is made worse if extra thick wire is used, because it cannot follow the curve of the roller easily.

To mitigate this, alter the length of wire on deck, by putting the loop on the end sometimes round the winch, sometimes on a cleat or bitts, and sometimes round a cleat with an athwart-ships lead to the winch, held by a lashing. Three different points on the wire will thus take turns at withstanding the nip of the roller. This technique should also be used where the moor-ing strop is of nylon or other fibre rope, to spread chafe.

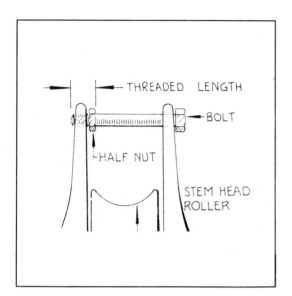

Never lost   Stemhead fittings incorporating a roller between vertical flanges are often manufactured without keep-pins; on others the pin lacks a chain to secure it to the fitting. The keep-pin suggested here is an ordinary non-rusting bolt which slides through a hole in the right-hand side and is threaded into the left-hand flange. To prevent it coming out completely a half nut is tightened up to the top of the thread so that when the gap is opened the pin only slides out as far as the half nut allows. Smearing paint around the thread of the half nut before it is tightened on the bolt will stop it vibrating loose, and when the nut has to be removed it is easy enough to break the seal.

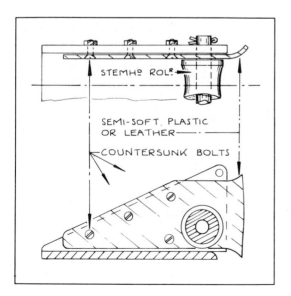

Warp protection   The current trend towards anchor ropes instead of chains has caught many manufacturers unawares. They are still making stemhead rollers with sharp forward edges on the side pieces. This has little effect on a chain, except to wear the galvanizing faster, but a warp will be cut through in a night. Padding round a warp stays put until everyone has turned in, then it wriggles up or down the rope, leaving it unprotected so that it chafes fast.

Adding permanent padding to the stemhead fitting is sometimes possible. The distance between the side pieces must remain sufficient to allow the home mooring chain to fit, even though the overnight anchor warp is much narrower than a chain. Countersunk fastenings should be used for preference, but if the padding material is thin, round-headed fastenings must be used, with washers.

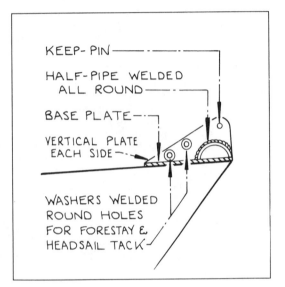

KEEP-PIN

HALF-PIPE WELDED
ALL ROUND

BASE PLATE

VERTICAL PLATE
EACH SIDE

WASHERS WELDED
ROUND HOLES
FOR FORESTAY &
HEADSAIL TACK

Stemhead fitting   For a boat under 25 ft
this is an easily made fitting which has the additional advantage of having no moving parts other
than the keep-pin through the tips of the side
plates.

   The whole fitting must be made of either
bronze or stainless steel since there is bound to
be wear on the half pipe and galvanizing would
soon wear off. Any softer material such as
Tufnol or nylon will wear away so quickly that it
will need renewing before the season ends.
The diameter of the half pipe should be as great
as possible to ease the effort of pulling in the
anchor chain or warp, and it must be of thick
gauge because there will be a certain amount
of wear over the years.

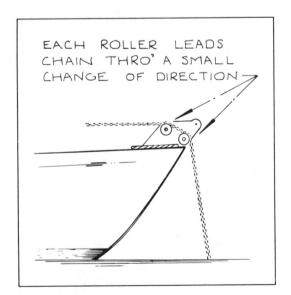

EACH ROLLER LEADS
CHAIN THRO' A SMALL
CHANGE OF DIRECTION

Chain rollers   If it is hard work pulling in
the anchor chain at least part of the reason is
likely to be the sharp turn which the chain makes
over the roller. The usual cure is to fit a larger
roller, but this is not always easy, for two
reasons. Chandlers rarely stock rollers larger
than about $2\frac{1}{2}$ in diameter, and it is not easy to fit
a big roller without quite enormous side
plates. If the stem is wood it may be cut away
somewhat to recess the roller, but a steel or
fibreglass hull cannot easily be cut away to drop
the roller down into the stemhead.

   An alternative is to fit two rollers so that each
leads the chain over about half the total angle.
There will be two points of friction, but as the
chain is lead fairly gradually over the bow
the total effort will be reduced. Both rollers
should have smooth axles and be well greased.

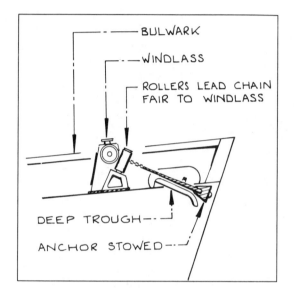

BULWARK

WINDLASS

ROLLERS LEAD CHAIN
FAIR TO WINDLASS

DEEP TROUGH

ANCHOR STOWED

Anchor stowage Anchors in hawsepipes
are the dream of many yacht owners. The ground
tackle stows itself when hauled home, and there
is not that maddening fight to get the ironware
inboard once it has been lifted : if the boat is
rolling it can be a dangerous game to get the
anchors stowed on deck. However, hawsepipes
are expensive and do not suit every hull form.

An alternative seen on a 100-tonner is a pair
of troughs. The starboard one is shown here
with the outboard side of the trough cut away
to show the anchor resting in the hauled-up
position. The bottom edge of the trough should
have a rolled lip or roller, so the chain runs in and
out smoothly. The anchor may need a little
levering to get it running out, and the trough
must be well forward to prevent the chain
fouling the stem.

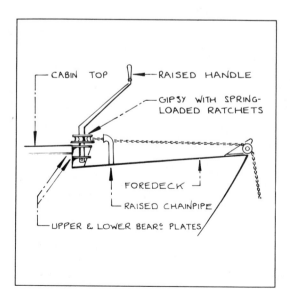

CABIN TOP

RAISED HANDLE

GIPSY WITH SPRING-
LOADED RATCHETS

FOREDECK

RAISED CHAINPIPE

UPPER & LOWER BEARG PLATES

Ratchet winch Seen on a 30 ft Dutch-built
steel yacht, this simple type of anchor winch is
easy to make and unusually cheap. It will
suit craft up to about 40 ft long.

The gypsy can be offset athwartships provided
the chain coming aft from the roller does not
foul the side plates of the stemhead fitting or
other deck gear. It is important that the chain
goes right round the gypsy before disappearing
down the chainpipe, otherwise there may be a
tendency for it to slip. The handle should be
made massive, and may have a ratchet incorporated provided this too is made very rugged.
Even though the chainpipe is raised off the deck
and faces aft it should have a hood or plug to
keep out water.

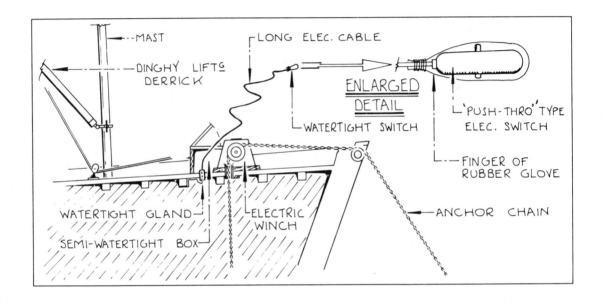

Remote control   One of the faults of electric
anchor winches is that the stop/start switch is
on or very close to the winch itself; anyone
bringing in an anchor cannot stand with his
hand on the control and at the same time see the
anchor as it comes to the surface. With a remote
control he can be right forward, looking over the
bow. It can also be used when bringing the
dinghy on board by using the winch to hoist
it on a derrick or davits.

To make the switch watertight it is encased
in a finger cut from a rubber glove; there is no
difficulty in switching on and off by pressing
through the rubber. A further idea is to have a
semi-watertight box behind the winch for
stowing the switch cable when not in use. The
box can also enclose the watertight deck gland,
keeping the heaviest water off it.

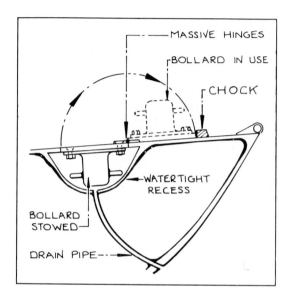

Pop-up bollard   The total development of fibreglass is still in its infancy. Years ago GRP cruisers came out with anchor lockers recessed below the foredeck so that the ironwork could be stowed out of sight. This gain in deck space has not generally been followed through. There is much to be said for fittings like the mooring bollard being so arranged, provided no strength is sacrificed. With the trend towards small cruisers and more enthusiastic racing, clear working space on the foredeck is in demand.

   Not only must a stowing bollard be fitted with substantial hinges, but there must also be a pair of rugged chocks, bolts or similar fastenings to brace the forward end when it is in the raised position—moving bollards can be a bit risky!

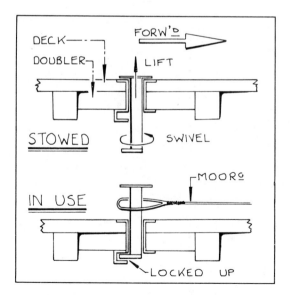

Bob-up bollard   This mooring post is suitable for boats like Dragons, Solings, Quarter Ton Cuppers and so on. Its main advantage is that when not in use it leaves the foredeck clear. The top plate is only about $\frac{1}{16}$ in thick and lies snug on the upper flange. The bollard itself is a well-fitted tube which slides inside the deck tube. It is important that the fit is good and the metal well greased to prevent water running down below. The top flange plate must be big enough to overlap the mooring chain or rope and the locking flange should extend round the tube about 180° so that the horizontal bar on the bottom of the main tube is unlikely to drop out.

   Typical dimensions for inshore racing boats of about 27 ft overall are: tube diameter $1\frac{1}{2}$ in, wall thickness $\frac{1}{8}$ in, height when raised 2 in above deck. From these sizes it will be appreciated that this is suitable for a sheltered mooring. The same fitting could be thickened up and enlarged for larger boats and for use on exposed moorings; however there is likely to be wear and play will develop if this style of fitting is over-stressed. As it is not likely to remain watertight if used hard, it is unlikely to be of general use for cruising yachts.

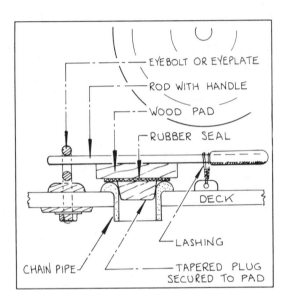

Deck plug   Whether alongside a winch or not, the chainpipe seldom has a watertight cover. If a tapered wood plug is made to go in the hole it is often hard to wedge it in place when the gypsy is located over the chainpipe. Even if a plug can be hammered in, it then becomes extremely difficult to remove. The sketch shows one way of making a plug which is quickly forced in place so securely that leaks are impossible, and yet is easy to remove. The plug is made with a wood flange and a rubber sealing washer. Over the top there is a rod or tube with a handle at one end and engaging in an eye at the other. As drawn the handle is forward, but it would be better the other way around on some boats. The rod can be made as long as necessary, so as to clear the whole winch.

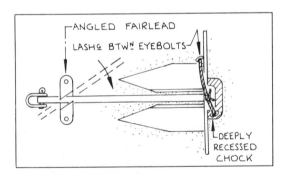

Anchor latch   An anchor on the foredeck is likely to be needed in a hurry. Also it has to be stowed quickly on many occasions, as the yacht leaves sheltered waters and buries her bow in the first wave at the harbour mouth. A complex arrangement of lashings to hold the pick to the deck is going to be neither popular, safe, nor easily released.

Here a fairlead holds the head of the stock, one of those metal bow fairleads with an angled slot. The anchor is laid down so that its stock drops into the mouth of the fairlead, then it is swivelled so that its stock drops into a deep recess in a hardwood chock. The anchor is kept from moving in any direction except upwards, which is taken care of by the single lashing and the arms of the fairlead.

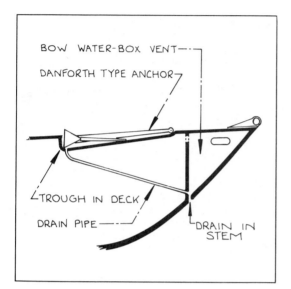

BOW WATER-BOX VENT

DANFORTH TYPE ANCHOR

TROUGH IN DECK

DRAIN PIPE

DRAIN IN STEM

Anchor recess   Anyone who has crewed on a yacht with a covered recess on the foredeck for the anchor will view the whole idea with mixed feelings. It is fine to have the whole of the deck uncluttered when handling headsails and warps, but coming to an anchorage things may be less satisfactory. The genoa is dropped and drapes itself over the lid which covers the anchor. The top itself gets in the way during subsequent operations, and is vulnerable to having its hinges (if any) damaged or to being blown or knocked overboard.

However, there is no need to have a cover over the anchor 'tray' provided a flat pattern of anchor is used. It can be set down about flush with the deck, and most of the area on and around the anchor can be walked over reasonably well.

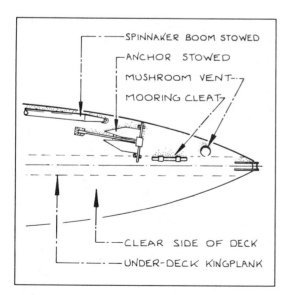

SPINNAKER BOOM STOWED

ANCHOR STOWED

MUSHROOM VENT

MOORING CLEAT

CLEAR SIDE OF DECK

UNDER-DECK KINGPLANK

Working and walking space   Though this idea was worked out for a trimaran, it applies to virtually any boat, especially if the deck is narrow. All the foredeck fittings (except stanchions) are located on one side. The other side is clear for getting up to the bow quickly.

Fittings like mooring cleats need a strong base so unless they are right at the edge of the deck they must be on the kingplank or whatever equivalent structure links the beams under the deck, and this restricts the distance that the cleat can be from the centreline. In any case it should not be too far from the stemhead roller, nor should there be anything between the stemhead and the cleat, otherwise the chain will not lead fair. It is also worth keeping the lead clear from the bow fairleads on each side to the mooring cleat. The same thinking can be applied when choosing an anchor winch, or deciding where to position a winch and navel pipe.

For a right-handed person it might be more convenient to have everything on the starboard side.

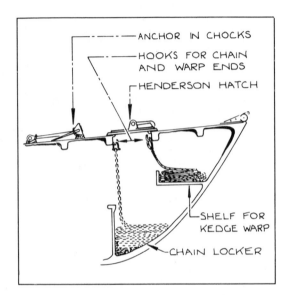

ANCHOR IN CHOCKS

HOOKS FOR CHAIN AND WARP ENDS

HENDERSON HATCH

SHELF FOR KEDGE WARP

CHAIN LOCKER

Watertight chainpipe   The anchor chain and kedge warp can be kept ready near the stem. One of the larger sizes of Henderson hatches is fitted on deck and there are thick bronze hooks, like coat-hooks, screwed to adjacent beams. When the hatch is closed it is completely watertight, which is important on any fast boat which throws up a lot of spray or takes water on deck. An ordinary chainpipe is seldom watertight, even with a plastic bag or hood lashed over it. It is important that the warp and chain are kept separate, except perhaps where there is just a short length of chain on the end of the only anchor warp carried. There is a temptation with this layout to use some form of snap shackle between the anchor and chain or warp, but the quick-release types of shackle are not strong and secure enough.

WARP PASSES THRO' FAIRLEAD

WARP SECURED TO CLEAT

WARP PASSES UNDER BEAM

CANVAS ANCHOR CRADLE

QUICK-RELEASE DEVICE ROUND FORWD BEAM

CRADLE FORE END DROPS TO RELEASE ANCHOR

Quick-release anchor   On a multihull it is not difficult to arrange for the anchor to live in a cradle between the forward crossbeams. If the aft edge of the cradle is permanently secured and the forward edge is made fast by a quickly released lacing or other device the anchor is easily let go. The warp is permanently led under the beam and may need half a dozen light seizings to keep it in place until needed. These will break when the anchor is let go. The quick-release mechanism can be a row of loops with a rod through them, or perhaps a Stenhouse clip.

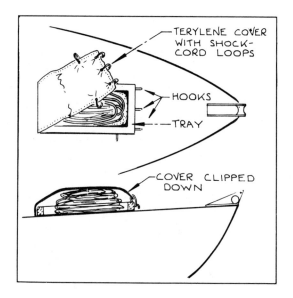

Kedge turtle   The idea of a spinnaker turtle may be applied to the stowage of the kedge warp or dock lines. The turtle may be permanent or portable; it is shown here as a tray with a wood rim all round, secured near the stem. To prevent the rope leaving the turtle there is a Terylene cover fastened across the aft end. Across the front and at each side there are tough shockcord loops which pass over hooks. The warp can be made fast to the anchor and the bitter end to the mooring bollard. In letting go the anchor it will be necessary only to unhook the forward loops on the cover. Provided the line is properly coiled it will run out on its own without snarling.

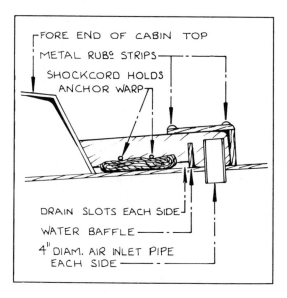

Deck box   Such a combined locker and ventilator might find favour on any cruiser, power or sail, inshore or offshore. A vertical coaming each side and at the forward end is built up ahead of the cabin top. It is partly covered over, both to keep the warp safe and to shield the vent inlet pipes. There can be two or three vents and if they are over 4 in in diameter they will provide a flow of air even in a zephyr.

The warp is coiled and held by shockcord straps stretched between the side coamings. When the warp is pulled out to let go the anchor it does not score the locker as there are protective metal strips on the edges. In severe conditions the shockcord will not be adequate on its own, and non-stretch lashings should be provided to secure the warp.

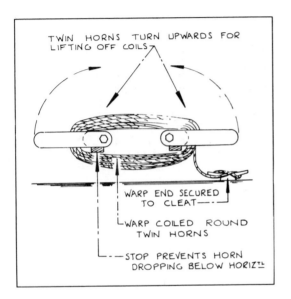

TWIN HORNS TURN UPWARDS FOR
LIFTING OFF COILS

WARP END SECURED
TO CLEAT

WARP COILED ROUND
TWIN HORNS

STOP PREVENTS HORN
DROPPING BELOW HORIZ.ᵗˡ

Safety stow   A kedge warp is needed in a hurry when a boat goes aground or enters harbour in a bit of a flurry. Other warps are often required just as urgently. If a long warp is stowed on a pair of horns which pivot upwards it can be stowed neatly yet remain ready for instant use. To grap the warp, just knock both horns into the vertical position and lift the warp off. To restow, lower the horns until they come up against the little chocks which form stops, and wind the warp round and round, having first made sure the bitter end is secured to prevent loss in extreme conditions.

The horns could be mounted on the foredeck, aft deck, below the forehatch, in the forepeak, or a forward cable locker on a multihull, at the aft end of the cockpit—in fact wherever rope stowage is required.

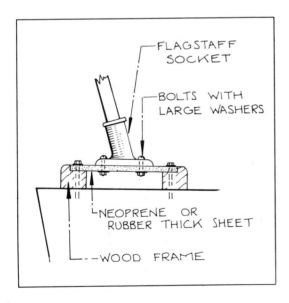

FLAGSTAFF
SOCKET

BOLTS WITH
LARGE WASHERS

NEOPRENE OR
RUBBER THICK SHEET

WOOD FRAME

Safe staff   More flagstaffs get broken than wear out. They protrude over the stern, delicate, unprotected and asking to be snapped off. The loss of the staff is infuriating enough, but when a prized flag disappears downtide with it, rage is sure to follow.

One way to make the staff more secure is to mount it on a flexible base. Rubber or neoprene which is thick enough to hold the staff in a gale but flexible enough to give to a firm nudge will be about $\frac{3}{8}$ in thick, though this will vary with the size of the yacht. (This thickness will suit a yacht about 40 ft long.) The bolts and nuts underneath the rubber should be at least $\frac{1}{2}$ in clear of the deck.

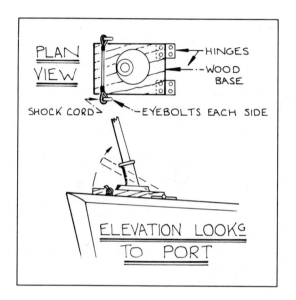

PLAN VIEW

HINGES

WOOD BASE

SHOCK CORD

EYEBOLTS EACH SIDE

ELEVATION LOOKᵍ TO PORT

Hinged flagstaff   This staff stands more chance than most in the scrum of a well-filled lock or dock. The essence of the idea is that the base of the flagstaff socket is pivoted and held down by shockcord. If the staff gets nudged, the baseboard hinges up and absorbs the shock. Admittedly this arrangement copes only with blows from aft—but that is the direction from which most of the trouble comes. It would not be difficult to put a rubber pad under the aft end of the staff, so that a thump from forward would be absorbed a little. The hinges and socket should be bolted to the board.

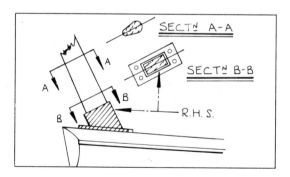

SECTᴺ A-A

SECTᴺ B-B

R.H.S.

Modern flagstaff   The traditional ensign staff is long, thin, round in section and vulnerable. It looks a bit Victorian and is more suited to the quieter days of the past. Although chandlers still only offer sockets which take round staffs, it is easy to make one up for a rectangular staff from a piece of rectangular hollow section steel or aluminium welded to a flat baseplate. After fabrication all the sharp edges should be ground off before the fitting is galvanized, epoxy painted and bolted to the deck. The staff is made a neat fit in the socket, but its upper part can be faired to a pear-shaped section, or at least the edges can be planed off thoroughly.

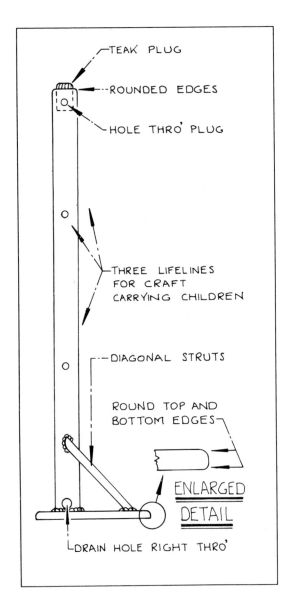

TEAK PLUG

ROUNDED EDGES

HOLE THRO' PLUG

THREE LIFELINES
FOR CRAFT
CARRYING CHILDREN

DIAGONAL STRUTS

ROUND TOP AND
BOTTOM EDGES

ENLARGED
DETAIL

DRAIN HOLE RIGHT THRO'

Special stanchions   There is not a great
choice then buying stanchions. For instance, it is
difficult to find them made of aluminium, or
with three lifeline holes, which are best for
yachts carrying children. Some people therefore
make their own from standard 1 in i.d. or 1 in
o.d. tubing welded to a $\frac{1}{4}$ in thick baseplate
about 4 in square. The end should be plugged
or else the wind will whistle in the most eerie
way as it blows over the top, and to reduce the
amount of water inside the tube. A turned teak
plug shrinks less than many other woods and
stays a tight fit. The top lifeline should pass
through the plug to prevent it from coming out
should it ever become loose, or be plucked at
by a sheet.

All edges of the stanchion tube and baseplate
must be well rounded off with a file or grinding
disc otherwise paint will chip off easily. If the
stanchion is made of mild steel it is important
to round the edges so that the galvanizing can
adhere properly. If edges are not ground rust is
likely to start there.

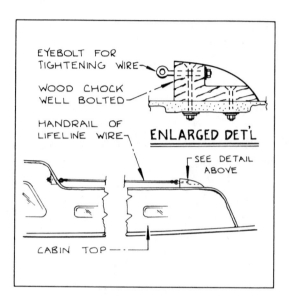

New line in lifelines   The usual cabin top handrail is a piece of 1 × 2 in teak, scalloped out and bolted down every 2 ft or so. This latest substitute has a number of advantages over the traditional pattern. It does not need varnishing annually, or even oiling. Like a jack-stay, it can be gripped at one end and the hand slid all the way forward without letting go. A safety harness line can be clipped on and slid along. It does not have many bolts through the cabin top, so there is less chance of leaks being started. It is light, offers little wind resistance, and is elegant because it is almost invisible.

The wire used should be the plastic covered type. It might well be given Norseman end terminals (which do not require special tools) with one end incorporating a rigging screw terminal. Alternatively, it can be tensioned by a lanyard.

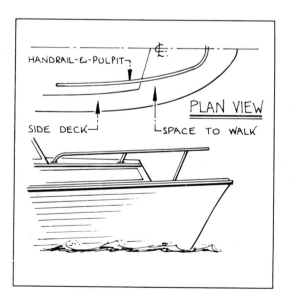

Safety rail   This combined pulpit and cabin top handrail is fitted on the Sagaling 30 footer. Its virtues are many, including: one rail from amidships forward so that the hand never has to be lifted off; strength because there are ample legs; smartness due to the long sweeping line; reliability since the pulpit does not overhang forward and risk damage alongside a dock.

Anyone going forward is outside the pulpit, but for most coastal cruising this is acceptable. The space outside the pulpit is just right for using a boathook, probably using one hand for the hook and the other on the rail. This rail is also economical, following the principle that where possible one fitting should serve two purposes or maybe even three.

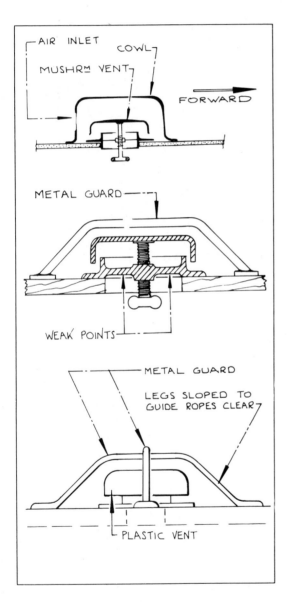

Mushroom vents   For boats which venture far afield an enveloping cowl over each mushroom vent helps to keep out stray spray. Of course it reduces ventilation, but if the boat lies in harbour for a long period the cowls can be removed. At sea, a small amount of fresh air uncontaminated by water is what the crew want, so the throttling effect of a partial cover over each vent is seldom important.

Mushroom vents made of certain types of plastic are found in service to be unreliable because they break at the weak points shown in the sketch. Even the weight of a young child standing on the cover will snap the axle support bar.

One notable disadvantage of this style of vent is its enthusiasm for snaring ropes, particularly headsail sheets. To defeat this bad habit a pair of guards with well-sloped legs should be fitted across the top of the vent. With luck and some care these guards will also prevent people from treading on the vent, so that the rather light plastic type may survive many seasons.

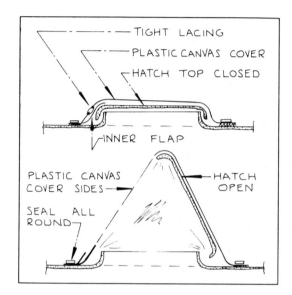

TIGHT LACING
PLASTIC CANVAS COVER
HATCH TOP CLOSED

INNER FLAP

PLASTIC CANVAS
COVER SIDES
HATCH OPEN

SEAL ALL ROUND

A persistent leaker   Some hatches are extremely difficult to make tight, especially if the hatch moulding and the deck or cabin top do not exactly match. One way round the problem is to make a canvas cover which is sealed all round except along the aft edge. Even here there is an upstanding lip or flap so that when the hatch is shut this lip is tight over the aft edge of the hatch top. After the hatch is closed the aft edge of the cover is laced tight over the flap. As the sides are protected from the weather the hatch can be kept open longer as the weather deteriorates. The canvas must of course be waterproof, impregnated with plastic or some similar material so that spray and rain run off it. For a prolonged passage the join could be further sealed by a run or two of sticky Sylglas glazing and bedding tape.

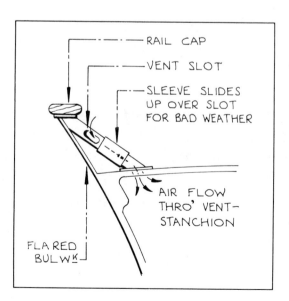

RAIL CAP
VENT SLOT
SLEEVE SLIDES UP OVER SLOT FOR BAD WEATHER

AIR FLOW THRO' VENT-STANCHION

FLARED BULWᴷ

Bulwark brace   Most bulwarks need support, especially if they follow a steeply raking flare. A functional, clean-lined stanchion which looks modern and has various practical features is shown here. It stands well clear of the scuppers, allowing water on deck to drain freely past. This in turn makes for easy cleaning of the scuppers, where so much grime from the deck tends to lodge if there are any obstructions. Tube is light for its strength, and both cheap and readily available. The idea of using the stanchions as ventilators is not new, but the method of closing the vent by a sliding sleeve is unusual. The vent slot should be near the top and facing aft, so it will not need closing until the weather really pipes up. Of course the sleeves should be checked fairly often to ensure that they have not seized up.

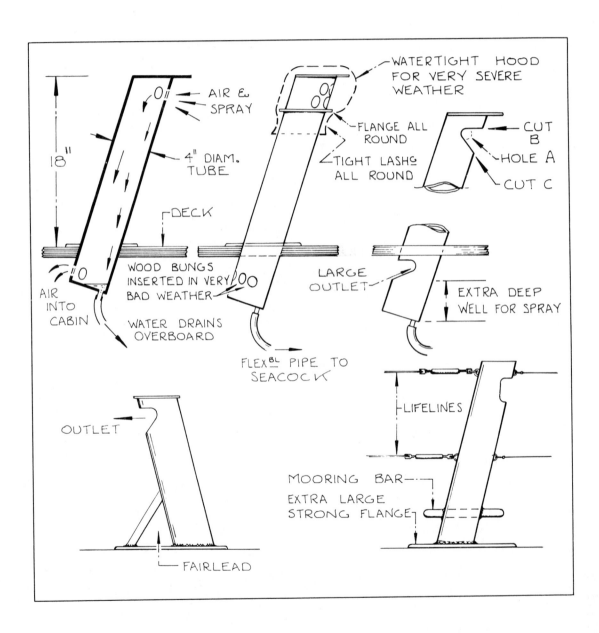

The straight pipe vent   This is a new
version of the water-box vent. It has the great
virtue of being effective yet extremely simple,
consisting of a straight tube with each end
blanked off, tilted to about 18° off the vertical.
Inlet holes are drilled at the top to let in the air
and again at the bottom. Since some spray is
likely to get in through the holes there is a drain
at the bottom which is joined by a flexible pipe
to the sea, possibly via the seacocks which cope
with water from the self-draining cockpit.
The top left hand picture shows the principle,
including the recommended dimensions. If the
tube is less than 18 in high it is likely to be in
the stagnant air near the deck and also more
likely to get solid water in it. Any tube of
less than 4 in diameter is not very effective at
promoting a good air flow.
   The middle top sketch shows how in very
bad conditions a watertight hood is lashed tightly
over the inlet and wood bungs pushed into the
holes at the bottom. An alternative form of inlet
and outlet is made by drilling a hole (A) right
through the tube and then making two cuts
(B) and (C) up to the hole (top right sketch).
This gives a much better flow of air but of course
is more likely to let in water in bad conditions.
If this type of outlet is used at the bottom it is
advisable to have an extra deep well in the
bottom to hold the spray so it has time to drain
overboard without slopping into the cabin.
   At the bottom are alternative designs, one
sloped back and used as an outlet, and having a
stiffening leg which forms an enclosed fairlead.
The other is in the form of a lifeline stanchion
with a mooring bar pushed through and welded
at each end. The deck flange has to be extra
strong to deal with the strain.

Cockpits and Wheelhouses

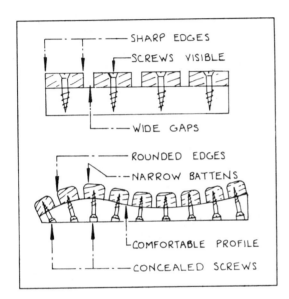

SHARP EDGES
SCREWS VISIBLE
WIDE GAPS

ROUNDED EDGES
NARROW BATTENS
COMFORTABLE PROFILE
CONCEALED SCREWS

Seat shape   Nobody likes sitting in a puddle, and on some modern yachts the fibreglass cockpit seats are cold and uncomfortable. If a grating, preferably of teak, is put on the seat it will dry out quickly and be more comfortable for long periods at the helm. The top sketch shows a rather crude type of slatted seat made without thought and lacking in elegance. The curved bottom design admittedly takes longer to make but greatly enhances the appearance of the yacht. Because the screws are driven upwards they are concealed. The outboard side is shown at the right and the profile can be copied from any comfortable park bench. (To copy a profile the simplest way is to cut a cardboard shape to match the required curve.)

A further possibility is shown in the bottom drawing. This might suit either power or sailing boats as it offers the helmsman support against the boat's motion or heeling. Such support is a great help in combating the fatigue of a long rough passage.

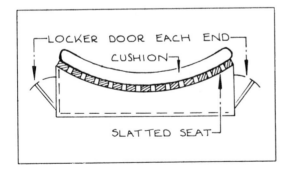

LOCKER DOOR EACH END
CUSHION
SLATTED SEAT

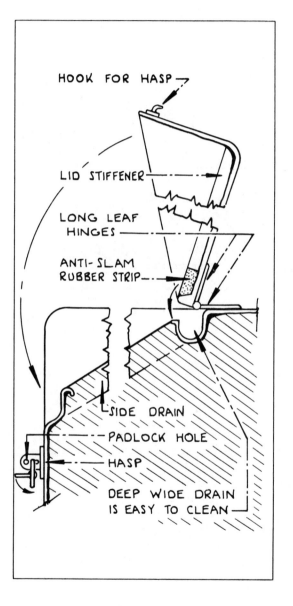

HOOK FOR HASP ⟶

LID STIFFENER

LONG LEAF HINGES

ANTI-SLAM RUBBER STRIP

SIDE DRAIN

PADLOCK HOLE

HASP

DEEP WIDE DRAIN IS EASY TO CLEAN

Cockpit locker lids   The lids of the lockers in this GRP cruiser are designed in such a way that they do not slam shut. A semi-hard rubber strip inside the outboard edge of the lid near the hinge catches on the inboard edge of the upper drain channel, and to close the locker a slight force has to be applied on top of the lid. The upper edge of the locker lid is thus most unlikely to leak since it has a water-tight seal, and because water is efficiently drained away by a large top drain and sloping side drains which are effective even when heeled.

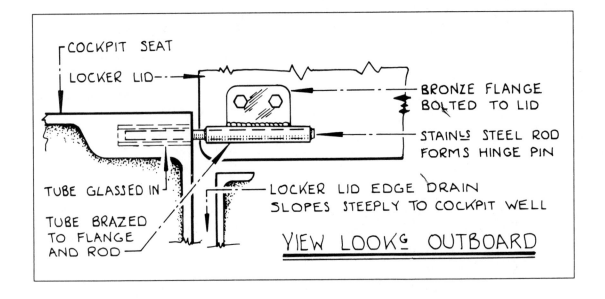

COCKPIT SEAT

LOCKER LID--

BRONZE FLANGE
BOLTED TO LID

STAIN̲S̲ STEEL ROD
FORMS HINGE PIN

TUBE GLASSED IN

TUBE BRAZED
TO FLANGE
AND ROD

LOCKER LID EDGE DRAIN
SLOPES STEEPLY TO COCKPIT WELL

VIEW LOOK̲S̲ OUTBOARD

Seat hinges   These cockpit locker hinges are totally concealed beneath the lid. The pins extend outwards, lodging in tubes glassed into the adjacent seat tops. One of the good features of this design is that only one side of the hinge is bolted on, bolts being unhappy bedfellows with fibreglass. Another is that a small amount of end play is worked in so that slight variations in seat size are automatically taken up. Lubrication is easy, and the hinge pins are extra strong.

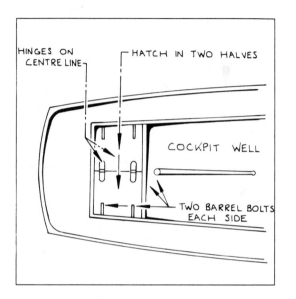

Lift-off hatch   There can scarcely be a yacht afloat which would not benefit on occasion from having a larger hatch, particularly when such unwieldy objects as sailbags are wanted from below, or that awkward outboard is needed in a hurry. Once at sea, though, there are plenty of times when a big hatch is an embarrassment. Its heavy lid takes two hands to lift, and there is a serious risk of pinched fingers.

On a Dutch yacht a clever compromise was seen. The hatch just aft of the tiller which gives access to the lazarette is in two halves. Both parts have barrel bolts holding them down but they share common hinges on the centreline. Either side can be unbolted and opened while for bulky objects both are lifted right off together.

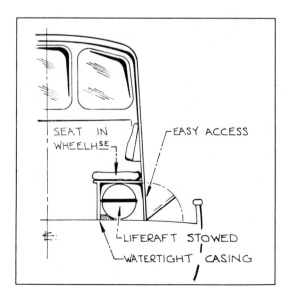

Liferaft locker   Although many yachts are now equipped with inflatable liferafts, designers have scarcely come to terms with this fairly new piece of equipment. As a result most rafts are just stuck on deck wherever there is space ; they get in the way, cause windage, are exposed to thieves, and sometimes get swept overboard.

A raft might be lodged safely in a special locker, recessed under a seat in the wheelhouse. The locker is watertight and made to be a neat fit for the encased raft. There must be space at one end to get a hand in to pull it out, or alternatively a rope or strap round the casing for pulling it out onto the side deck. It may well be that the type of raft which is in a rectangular container will fit more conveniently.

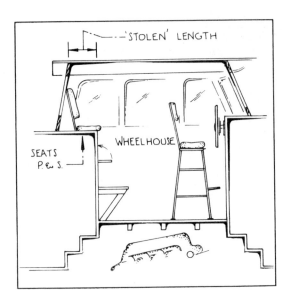

Stolen space   A characteristic of converted fishing vessels such as MFVs, and some older motor cruisers, is lack of space in the wheelhouse. Since the whole crew likes to collect in the wheelhouse, at least when on passage, any scheme which gives a little more space is popular. The aft end of a wheelhouse can be extended to give extra sitting space. Naturally there are problems, such as adequate headroom between the wheelhouse deckhead and the aft cabin top. Also anybody sitting on the new aft seat needs a footrest. Folding footrests could be the answer, or the lower seat may act as a footrest. A grabrail in the deckhead, and perhaps arms on the sides of the seat, will protect anyone from being thrown about in rough conditions.

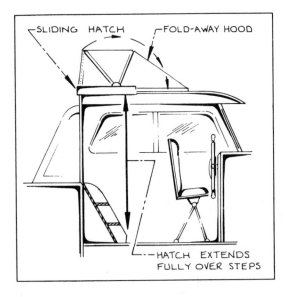

Dry in the rain   Another idea for increasing the effective space in the wheelhouse is shown here. The sliding hatch increases headroom and makes moving between the after cockpit or deck and the wheelhouse easier, and in fine weather or at anchor allows more light and ventilation.

Gently sloping steps require a correspondingly long hatchway to give headroom, but for children and smaller people a long hatch may be too heavy to close easily: the canopy is light in weight and adequate in most conditions. Neither the hatch nor the folding 'pram hood' canopy spoil the integrity of the wheelhouse structure if properly made.

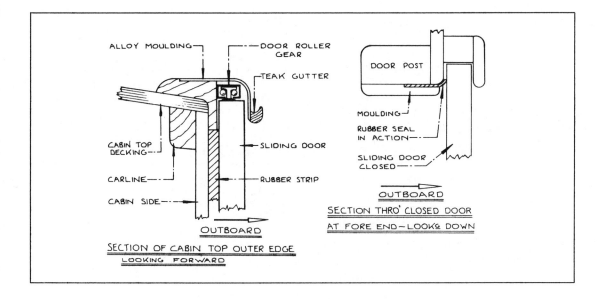

ALLOY MOULDING

DOOR ROLLER GEAR

TEAK GUTTER

DOOR POST

MOULDING

RUBBER SEAL IN ACTION

SLIDING DOOR CLOSED

CABIN TOP DECKING

CARLINE

CABIN SIDE

SLIDING DOOR

RUBBER STRIP

OUTBOARD

OUTBOARD

SECTION THRO' CLOSED DOOR AT FORE END—LOOKS DOWN

SECTION OF CABIN TOP OUTER EDGE LOOKING FORWARD

Sliding doors   The pair of sketches shows a wheelhouse door arrangement which is easy to open and close, yet weatherproof. The roller gear is an industrial type. A standard aluminium moulding edged with a specially made teak gutter throws rain and spray clear of the door. When closed, a wide rubber strip is pushed sideways to form a seal.

If a sliding door is fitted between an upper and lower grooved wood channel it will seldom behave properly; it is likely to jam, and when it does move to be jolty and difficult.

Various forms of sliding door hardware are available but many are unsuited to marine use, since they are likely to corrode and seize up. Alternatively, a normal mainsheet traveller and track can be set upside down and used to carry a door. The weight of even a heavy door is nothing like the strain the sheet traveller must normally withstand, but there may be problems in adapting it to fit onto the door. It will almost certainly be necessary to have two travellers on the track, one at each edge of the door.

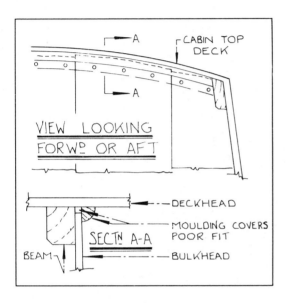

VIEW LOOKING FORWᴰ OR AFT

SECTᴺ A-A

A joggly join   A bulkhead may be made up of strips of wood or wide pieces of plywood, or other seawater-resistant boarding. There is always the problem of obtaining a neat finish between the top of the bulkhead and the decking. It may be best to admit that the job is beyond the bounds of available skill and simply make a reasonably good fit, covering the join with a strip of quarter-round moulding. The join should still be made as tight as possible so that there is a good landing for the bulkhead on the beam, and because if the job is done too carelessly the moulding may be inadequate to cover the rough edges. It is also important to make sure that the moulding available can follow the camber of the deck, before using this technique.

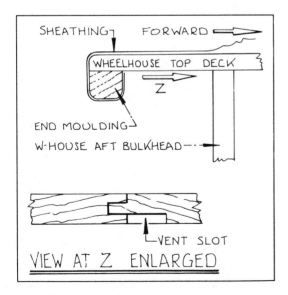

VIEW AT Z ENLARGED

Tiny vents   Some tongue-and-groove boards have decorative recesses machined into them when the tongue is cut out. If this type of boarding is used for covering a wheelhouse top it makes sense to put the recess on the underside. The little slots where the deck meets the bulkhead may be left open as ventilator slots provided there is ample overhang to prevent rain and spray getting in.

Tongue-and-groove boarding has to be covered with some form of sheathing to make it watertight, so the top deck may be extended far enough to wrap the sheathing round the edge. A moulding across the deck boards is essential, not only for strength but also to give the sheathing a proper finish. Sheathing should not be wrapped round a sharp edge, so the plank ends and the moulding are both well rounded.

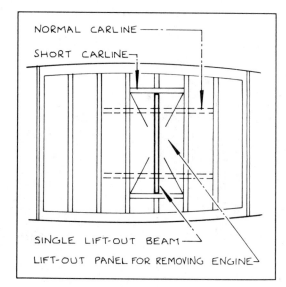

NORMAL CARLINE

SHORT CARLINE

SINGLE LIFT-OUT BEAM

LIFT-OUT PANEL FOR REMOVING ENGINE

Wheelhouse beams   It is common practice to arrange for a portable panel in the top of a wheelhouse or steering shelter to allow the engine to be lifted clear of the boat. As engines are installed with their crankshafts fore and aft the panel is made longer in that direction. The trouble is that this involves cutting through several beams and weakening the structure, which is sometimes not particularly strong anyway, and may have to support a radar or liferaft.

Since the engine is lifted out by a tackle or crane it can usually be rotated 90° once it is clear of the engine compartment and lifted through the roof of the deckhouse with the crankshaft athwartships. Logically, therefore, the clever thing to do is to make the panel short and wide.

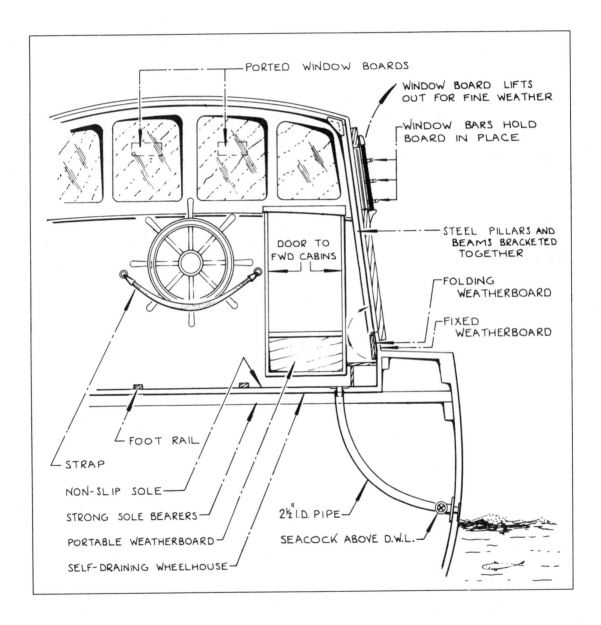

PORTED WINDOW BOARDS

WINDOW BOARD LIFTS OUT FOR FINE WEATHER

WINDOW BARS HOLD BOARD IN PLACE

STEEL PILLARS AND BEAMS BRACKETED TOGETHER

DOOR TO FWD CABINS

FOLDING WEATHERBOARD

FIXED WEATHERBOARD

FOOT RAIL

STRAP

NON-SLIP SOLE

STRONG SOLE BEARERS

PORTABLE WEATHERBOARD

SELF-DRAINING WHEELHOUSE

2½" I.D. PIPE

SEACOCK ABOVE D.W.L.

Weather-worthy   It is only necessary to compare a lifeboat with a yacht to see that relatively few power craft are truly suitable for vicious weather. The sketch shows a few improvements, some of which could be incorporated in almost any craft to make her more seaworthy.

All the big wheelhouse windows are fitted with strong, portable, ply weatherboards. Some, if not all, have slots to give visibility. The weatherboards can be fitted by dropping them inside the bars over the windows, and some form of turnbutton or catch is needed to keep each board in place.

To keep water out there is normally some sort of sill at the deckhouse door. This can be greatly improved by having a hinged section which lodges tight against the side coamings and helps to keep out deep water running along the deck. Any water that gets into the wheelhouse can be prevented from going below by a built-in coaming or portable weatherboard at each entrance to the interior of the yacht. However, these are not much good if they are not fitted in conjunction with a watertight sole. In this sketch the sole has a large drain each side leading to a seacock located *above* the waterline. In the event of a seacock failure the yacht will not sink on moorings. Naturally if the sole is going to carry a lot of water it must be strong enough to support this weight, and extra stout beams fitted across the yacht amidships are always an asset.

To make life more comfortable for the helmsman he may be given a strap such as is sometimes fitted in the galley, to go round his waist or bottom and prevent him from being thrown about. At his feet he needs wood cleats so that he can jam each foot securely in place and not slither about.

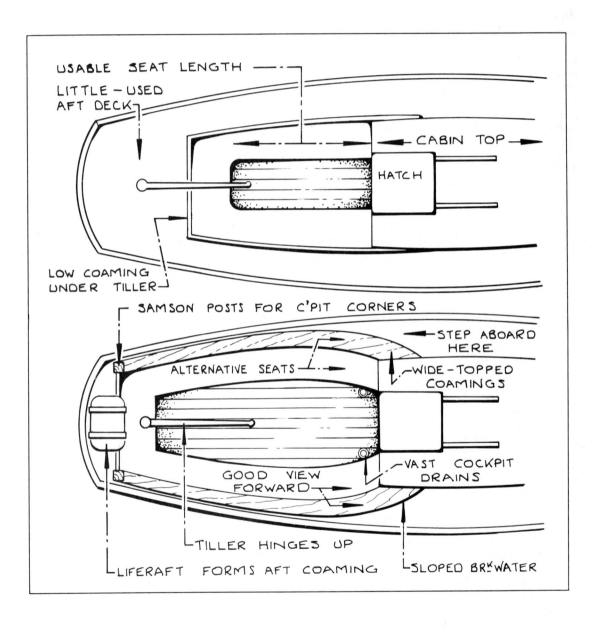

USABLE SEAT LENGTH

LITTLE – USED
AFT DECK

CABIN TOP

HATCH

LOW COAMING
UNDER TILLER

SAMSON POSTS FOR C'PIT CORNERS

STEP ABOARD
HERE

ALTERNATIVE SEATS

WIDE – TOPPED
COAMINGS

GOOD VIEW
FORWARD

VAST COCKPIT
DRAINS

TILLER HINGES UP

LIFERAFT FORMS AFT COAMING

SLOPED BRKWATER

More space in the cockpit   A big
difference between boats built now and those
made twenty years ago is in the foot room and
sitting space in their cockpits. One way to
modernize an old boat is to increase the cockpit
area. Here the cockpit coamings have been
pushed right out almost to the deck edge and
the aft end of the cockpit has been taken a
long way back. No change has been suggested
for the main cabin top and its hatch because this
tends to be more expensive and complicated. The
cockpit coamings are made in box sections so
that the crew can sit on top of them with a
good view forward. In bad weather they will
probably sit on the ordinary cockpit seats which
have been pushed further outboard and extended
aft. On moorings, when having a party on board,
the tiller will be hinged up vertically and possibly
lashed to the backstay to keep it out of the way.

   Of course there are some disadvantages. For
instance, the cockpit becomes more vulnerable
and it is essential to have high coamings to
keep out breaking seas. Since the aft coaming is
no longer underneath the tiller it can be much
higher and might be further raised by incorporating the liferaft as part of the coaming. The side
coamings must be swept in at the forward end
to divert water away from the cockpit. Since the
well is much bigger it must have really vast
drains to get rid of water as quickly as possible.
Although one effect of the alterations is that
the helmsman and crew should have a better
view forward, it may be necessary to put a
dinghy-type extension on the tiller.

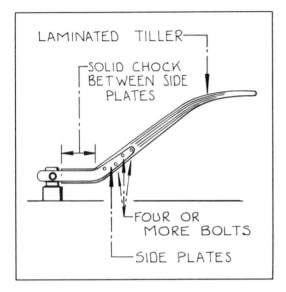

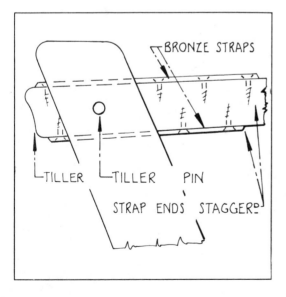

Laminated tillers   Where it is necessary to put a double bend in a tiller it is seldom possible to get a piece of wood with the precise sweeps and curves in the grain. It is usual to use a laminated tiller in this situation, but the reverse bend may present some problems especially as it is vital to ensure that the layers of wood are perfectly glued, otherwise the athwartships bolts will split them apart.

An ingenious trick is to make up a laminated tiller with a single bend by the handgrip, and extend the rudder side straps to embrace a solid chock of wood as well as the bottom section of the laminated part. In effect the metal straps make up the strength members of the bottom bend, with the wood forming a spacer and filler.

The same general approach can be used if a laminated tiller breaks. Instead of making up a completely new tiller a new filler piece is shaped from matching hardwood. The join may be glued, but its strength will chiefly be in the new side plates. These will be about $\frac{1}{4}$ in thick for a 35 ft boat and about $\frac{1}{8}$ in thick for a 25-footer, with the maximum depth. At least three bolts each side of the join are needed and five each side are best. Screws are never tolerable in such an important component.

If there is any doubt about the strength of the side plates or the joins additional plates can be put on the top and bottom of the tiller. All the plates should have plenty of thickness, but can have lightening holes where weight is a serious consideration. Straps could also be used to stiffen a tiller before it breaks, close to the rudderhead but with the ends of the straps staggered to avoid an abrupt change in stiffness that will encourage breaking. Bronze is recommended for the straps.

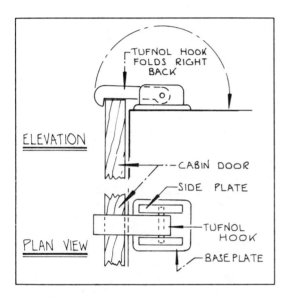

ELEVATION

─ TUFNOL HOOK
  FOLDS RIGHT
  BACK

─ ─ CABIN DOOR

─ SIDE PLATE

PLAN VIEW

─ TUFNOL
  HOOK

─ BASE PLATE

Gravity door catch   The two companion-way doors on a cruiser could have this simple securing clip made from Tufnol with a brass pivot. The hooks are fitted on the aft end of the cabin top so that when the doors are swung right open the clips catch the top edge and hold them in place. Each clip consists of a hook on a pivot held between two upright plates (again of Tufnol) all on a baseplate of the same material. When the doors are shut each hook folds forward out of the way. This idea could be adapted to hold a toilet door closed or a fore-hatch shut. If the doors do not open right against the bulkhead, the hook may be made longer and hold the door against a rubber stop.

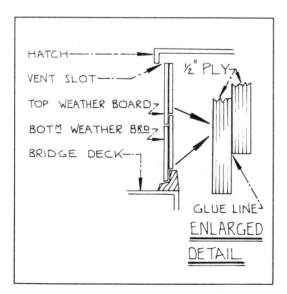

HATCH ─ ─ ─ ─ ─ ─

VENT SLOT ─ ─ ─

TOP WEATHER BOARD ─

BOT^M WEATHER BRD ─

BRIDGE DECK ─ ─ ─

½" PLY

GLUE LINE

ENLARGED
DETAIL

Watertight weather boards   This type of weather board is made by gluing two layers of ply together. On small, light boats each piece of ply might be $\frac{5}{16}$ in thick, but for normal sea use $\frac{1}{2}$ in or even thicker. For ocean cruising the ply pieces should be $\frac{3}{4}$ in or even thicker.

The two layers glued together give a step at the bottom which excludes water even when a moderate wave breaks against the weather boards. The depth of the step need not be great; 1 in is adequate. All edges should be rounded slightly and there must be enough clearance for the boards to slide into place easily even after they have been given four coats of varnish, and to allow for any distortion of the opening.

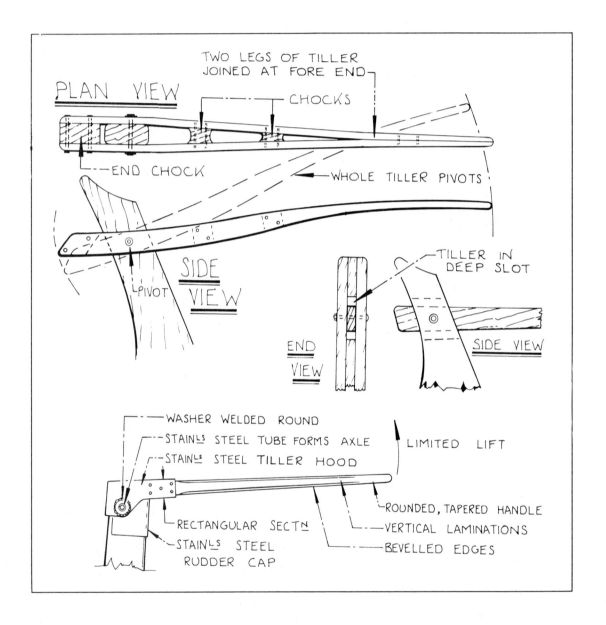

PLAN VIEW

TWO LEGS OF TILLER
JOINED AT FORE END
CHOCKS
END CHOCK
WHOLE TILLER PIVOTS

SIDE VIEW
PIVOT

TILLER IN DEEP SLOT
END VIEW
SIDE VIEW

WASHER WELDED ROUND
STAINLS STEEL TUBE FORMS AXLE
STAINLS STEEL TILLER HOOD
LIMITED LIFT
RECTANGULAR SECTN
ROUNDED, TAPERED HANDLE
VERTICAL LAMINATIONS
STAINLS STEEL RUDDER CAP
BEVELLED EDGES

Adjustable tillers A tiller which can be raised out of the way makes the cockpit much bigger. The whole of the area is then available for living space when at anchor, and where there is an engine hatch in the cockpit access will be much improved.

A two-legged tiller which straddles the rudder head can be tilted through a wide angle, whereas the pattern shown just below it is limited by the depth of slot and can be angled only a few degrees. The design at the bottom has a very strong connection to the rudderhead and a limited but adequate lift.

Whatever arrangement is chosen, all compon-ents should be really strong and apparently oversize for the length of the boat. A tiller must be entirely free from knots and other flaws, typical woods being mahogany, occasionally teak, sometimes oak.

Engines and Systems

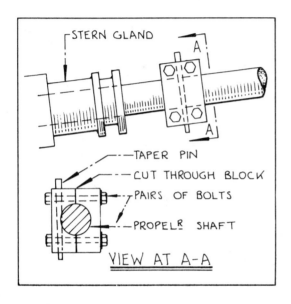

STERN GLAND

A

A

TAPER PIN

CUT THROUGH BLOCK

PAIRS OF BOLTS

PROPELᴿ SHAFT

VIEW AT A-A

Shaft stop   To stop a propeller shaft pulling out by accident, a block can be clamped to it just ahead of the stern gland. One way of making this is to drill a hole the size of the shaft diameter through a steel chock. The chock is then cut in half and the two halves bolted together round the shaft. The saw cut is quite enough to make the chock fit tightly on the shaft. As a further precaution a hole can be drilled through the chock to indent the chock by about 5% of its diameter; a taper pin is then driven through to lock the two together. The stop could also be made of hardwood, and the corners rounded off for safety whatever material is used..

This safety stop may seem an unnecessary precaution, but in one period of six months in my area four shafts pulled out. Because of the size of the hole left when the shaft disappears astern it is not always easy to plug quickly.

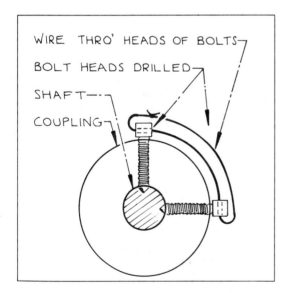

WIRE THRO' HEADS OF BOLTS

BOLT HEADS DRILLED

SHAFT

COUPLING

Unshakeable coupling   Where there are no keyways to lock them to propeller or rudder shafts, couplings are usually held with metal thread screws, sometimes in the form of Allen screws. If these are not secured, vibration may work them free. To make them safe the heads should be drilled and a wire passed through all the heads. Some Allen screws will be the recessed type and it will be impossible to lock their heads with wire; the recessed type should be replaced by those with the head clear of the coupling perimeter.

It is bad practice to rely on only one of these screws, but in cases where only one has been fitted it can still be wired up, the wire passing round the shaft as well as through the head.

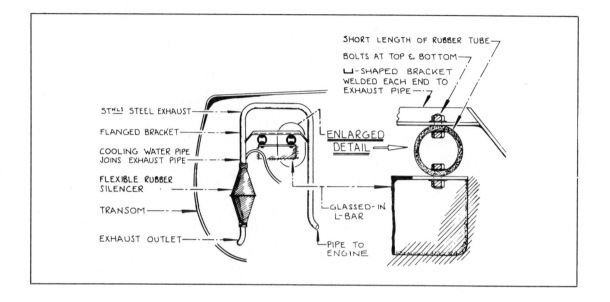

SHORT LENGTH OF RUBBER TUBE
BOLTS AT TOP & BOTTOM
⊔-SHAPED BRACKET
WELDED EACH END TO
EXHAUST PIPE

STₙᴸˢ STEEL EXHAUST
FLANGED BRACKET
COOLING WATER PIPE
JOINS EXHAUST PIPE
FLEXIBLE RUBBER
SILENCER
TRANSOM
EXHAUST OUTLET

ENLARGED
DETAIL

GLASSED-IN
L-BAR
PIPE TO
ENGINE

Exhaust mountings In order to isolate the vibrating exhaust from the hull two very simple flexible couplings are used here. They are made from short lengths of rubber hose, the top being bolted to the exhaust support bracket and the bottom to a glassed-in angle-bar. In a 25 ft boat 3 in lengths of common reinforced rubber tubing of about $1\frac{1}{2}$ in diameter would normally be about right. Any faults can be easily repaired, and if the rubber couplings perish or become damaged they can be replaced with easily available material.

The flexible rubber silencer absorbs vibration in the exhaust system, as well as reducing engine noise. This type of silencer also prevents water flooding back, as does the high loop in the exhaust pipe. In this installation there is virtually no chance of the engine being flooded by seawater during heavy weather.

Funnel vent   Some ideas can be borrowed from big ships. For instance, few yachts have funnels, yet such a structure has more than one use. A modern exhaust uptake is often built into the mast with a ventilator or two combined in the trunking.

The side of the funnel has been cut away here to show the interior. The air inlet is covered to keep away rain, and some form of baffle to exclude spray may be needed. The exhaust vent is similar; in practice one of the two should be ducted right into the bilge otherwise the air will simply take a short cut out, doing no good. Locating the silencer in the funnel puts this bulky item out of the way and keeps heat out of the interior.

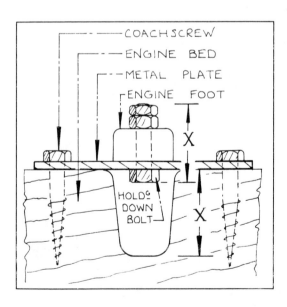

Awkward engine beds   Ideally every engine foot should be bolted down, though on some boats it is impossible to do this for reasons which vary from inaccessibility to lack of depth. Common practice is to use coach screws in this situation, but these are not entirely reliable. There are few alternatives, so it is sensible to make the best of a bad situation by doubling or even trebling the number of coach screws.

The metal plate should be thick, and as wide or wider than the bearer. The recess for the engine holding-down bolt is made deep enough to allow the bolt to be put in upwards, and should allow room for a socket to grip the bolt head. It is essential to put on a locking nut as well as the main nut.

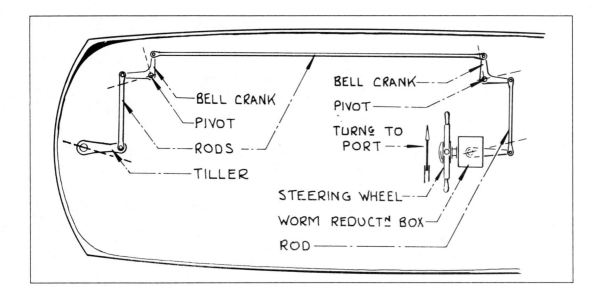

Smooth steering   Rod steering tends to be
smoother than linkages made from lengths of
wire, or chain. Rod does not stretch or strand
like wire, nor is it necessary to leave the
amount of slack which wire steering demands
if it is not to be too tight for easy handling
and effortless turning of the helm.

Rod systems are often based on a worm
reduction gearbox such as those made by Fenner
or Croft, or even a truck steering box. The rod is
made to turn corners by fitting bell cranks, which
can also be designed to give extra leverage by
varying the crank lengths. When designing an
assembly like this it is no bad thing to draw
some of the bell crank arms overlength with
alternative holes. Then the 'feel' and power of
the steering can be adjusted during trials by
moving the rod ends to different holes. The
dotted lines in the sketch show the movement
of the components in the system when the

wheel is turned to port.

Long rods need roller supports, usually at
about 6 ft intervals, to prevent sagging or bending under compressive strains. All joins should
be assembled with plenty of grease and more
put in after every 500 hours' use. Every few
years the linking pins will need renewing, but if
well greased they will last a long time. Grease
nipples at the pivots are worth having to
minimize wear and increase reliability.

A side advantage of rod steering is that it
tends to be quiet; it certainly is reliable, and
perhaps its weakness is that it lasts so long that
failure sometimes occurs when a rod rusts
through.

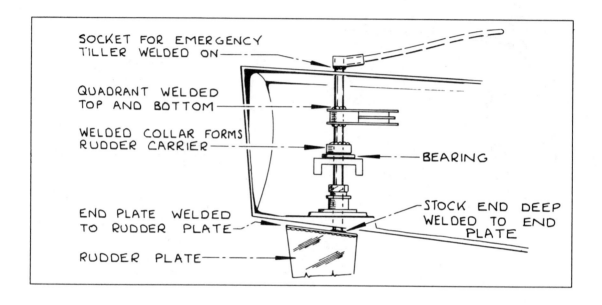

SOCKET FOR EMERGENCY
TILLER WELDED ON——

QUADRANT WELDED
TOP AND BOTTOM——

WELDED COLLAR FORMS
RUDDER CARRIER——

BEARING

END PLATE WELDED
TO RUDDER PLATE——

STOCK END DEEP
WELDED TO END
PLATE

RUDDER PLATE——

All-welded stock   The traditional rudder stock is not made in ten minutes. It has a square machined head for the quadrant and the emergency tiller; there may be a single or double keyway for the rudder carrier collar; the bottom may be machined to straddle the rudder plate. An all-welded fabrication has many advantages: for a start it is much quicker to make and assemble, and since each component is welded in position nothing is likely to work loose at sea, unless it has been made under-strength or not properly welded. The main disadvantage is that repair can only be carried out by cutting off welded components for dismantling. In practice this can be a good thing because it ensures that worn parts will not be reused. It is usually quicker to cut off steel parts than to dismantle them, particularly if they have become worn or rusty or are located in corners. However, if anything does go wrong at sea repairs can be uncommonly awkward.

The end plate on the steel rudder should increase its efficiency by preventing water flow over the top of the blade.

Simpler stock   The top of a rudder stock is normally machined square to take the quadrant and emergency tiller. Machining is seldom a quick job, and is less generally available than welding. If the top of the stock is cut diagonally and a rectangular or square section bar welded on, it will take the quadrant and tiller conveniently. One diagonal cut only is needed across the flat bar for the piece on top and the piece on the bottom (see adjacent sketch) which saves a little work. Naturally the welding must be beyond reproach, and the top pieces of bar aligned very carefully. The quadrant is usually made in two halves and clamped on. It does not always have a bolt through the stock, but where there is sufficient metal left after drilling, it is worth having.

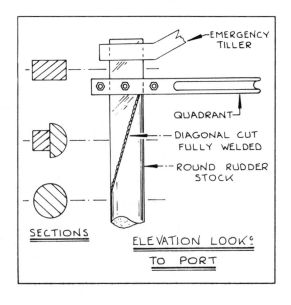

SECTIONS

ELEVATION LOOK^g TO PORT

EMERGENCY TILLER
QUADRANT
DIAGONAL CUT FULLY WELDED
ROUND RUDDER STOCK

Simpler rudder   When making up a rudder it is not uncommon to wrap two plates round the stock and fasten through. The stock is machined to a taper at the bottom, both to narrow the bottom of the blade and to ensure that the two plates grip a flat surface. This relieves the load on the bolts or clenches, otherwise they alone would be resisting the stock's tendency to turn inside the two plates. To eliminate the slow, costly machining the stock is made up of a conventional round bar, but the bottom part is of thick flat bar. As the join is a long diagonal cut, the weld (on both sides) is long and strong, and there are no sudden changes of section. The round bar is ground away near its bottom to facilitate fitting the rudder plates. The sketch below shows a simple complementary rudder stock arrangement.

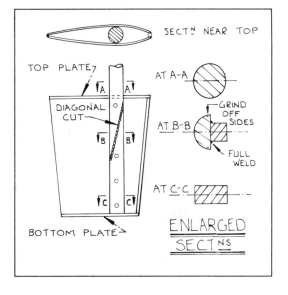

SECT^N NEAR TOP
TOP PLATE
DIAGONAL CUT
AT A-A
AT B-B   GRIND OFF SIDES
FULL WELD
AT C-C
BOTTOM PLATE
ENLARGED SECT^{NS}

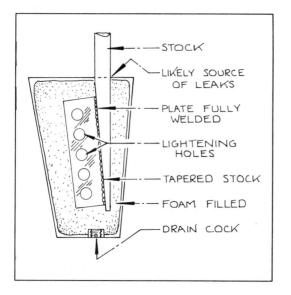

STOCK

LIKELY SOURCE
OF LEAKS

PLATE FULLY
WELDED

LIGHTENING
HOLES

TAPERED STOCK

FOAM FILLED

DRAIN COCK

Rudder construction   Fibreglass boats
often have rudders of the same material, and
sometimes damaged rudders are replaced by
moulded ones made up specially. They can be
made in a variety of ways and some of the
design details which may be incorporated are
listed here.

It is usual to have a bronze or stainless steel
stock, and a plate or rods can be welded to this.
The welding should be perfect and continuous.
The plate can have a number of quite large
lightening holes cut out as it need not bear
everywhere on the rudder sides. It is common
but not universal to make the rudder up in two
halves with the join vertically down the
centreline. This leaves a weakness where the
stock enters, so leaking here must be expected :
thus there is a drain hole, since any foam filling
can not be entirely relied on to exclude water.
The drain plug, which is flush, should be unscrewed each winter.

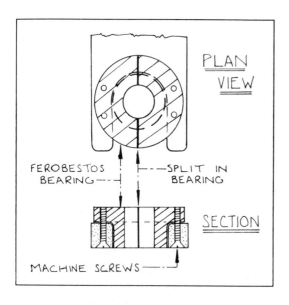

PLAN
VIEW

FEROBESTOS
BEARING

SPLIT IN
BEARING

SECTION

MACHINE SCREWS

Bottom bearing   A rudder bearing which
cannot easily be renewed is an expensive
nuisance. The design shown is particularly
simple and can be renewed without taking the
rudder or any other fittings off. The bearing is
machined, then cut in half and reamed out so
that the rudder heel stub fits exactly. It does not
matter if the outside circumference is not perfectly circular. One half of the bearing is
slipped in place and rotated until it is ahead
of the rudder. This allows the second part to be
fitted in, and then the two halves are rotated
until the join runs fore and aft. Machine screws
are then threaded into both the heel fitting and
the bearing material.

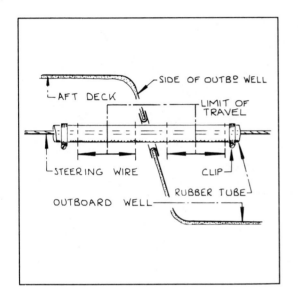

Outboard steering wire   It is usual on an outboard runabout to have a separate well for the engine. The sides of this well are pierced with holes through which the steering wire passes. Unfortunately the wires often foul the edges of the holes and sometimes wear away the grommets. The holes have to be made fairly large so that the wires lead through easily, but this does mean that water slopping up into the well may lap into the main part of the hull.

If rubber or plastic sleeves are put on the wires at the holes, wear will be reduced and the amount of water which can get through the holes is limited. The tubing must be secured firmly to the wire, possibly with hose clamps. Care must be taken that the tubing and clamps extend beyond the limit of the travel, otherwise they will catch.

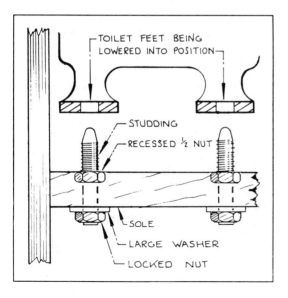

Bolting down the toilet   Virtually all makes of w.c. have their feet tucked in close under the bowl, so that it is very hard to get the bolts in. A technique that works well in cramped corners is to pencil through the bolt holes in the feet, then remove the w.c. and drill through the sole—which itself must be well secured. Next put studding through the holes. Studding is rod which is threaded throughout its length and in this case should be of brass or bronze. Big washers with locking nuts are put on the bottom and the tops are filed to blunt points so that the w.c. feet are more easily located. Half-nuts are run down the studding and countersunk flush in the sole so that when the w.c. is lowered in place the studding is locked firmly and the w.c. has a solid fastening.

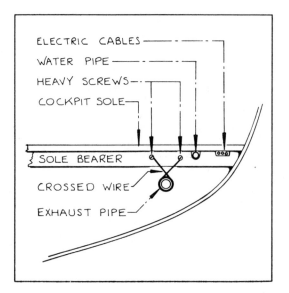

ELECTRIC CABLES
WATER PIPE
HEAVY SCREWS
COCKPIT SOLE
SOLE BEARER
CROSSED WIRE
EXHAUST PIPE

Pipe hangers   Before the cockpit sole was laid the tops of the bearers were recessed for pipes and electrical cables. The cut-away sections of the bearers were well outboard so that the loss of strength was tolerable. To secure the exhaust pipes strong round-headed screws were put in to hold loops of wire. Though each support is small, together they are more than adequate to hold the pipe. Also, being small, they do not transmit much heat up to the wooden bearer, so there is no risk of charring. The exhaust pipe is hung well below the sole, with plenty of air circulating around it. Close-spaced support for pipes and cables is achieved without buying cable clips or pipe hangers.

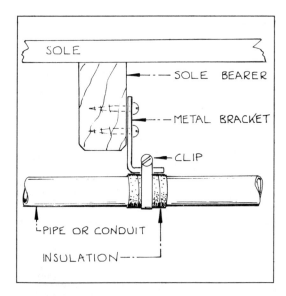

SOLE
SOLE BEARER
METAL BRACKET
CLIP
PIPE OR CONDUIT
INSULATION

Pipe holder   This method of securing pipes is cheap, quick to fit and can be used with every sort of tube, rod, control cable, conduit and even electric wiring. The insulation is desirable in almost every case and may be essential in some since it is probable that the bracket and the pipe will be of different metals. As there is likely to be bilgewater splashing up on the bracket, some sort of electrolytic action will occur if different metals or alloys are in contact. It may be slight, but a little insulation can so often prevent a lot of irritating trouble in an out-of-the-way area. It also serves as padding and a vibration absorber, if a somewhat spongy, thick material is used.

Brackets should be fitted at every sole bearer, because it is almost impossible to over-do the number of pipe supports—most yachts suffer from a shortage of them. Ideally there should be three or more screws in each bracket.

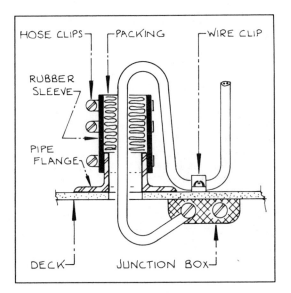

HOSE CLIPS ┌PACKING   ┌WIRE CLIP

RUBBER
SLEEVE

PIPE
FLANGE

DECK   JUNCTION BOX

Cable gland   Where electric appliances and lights are needed on deck, it is usual to have a plug and socket near the fitting. However these so-called watertight plugs are often neither sea nor rain proof. A better idea is to lead a wire direct from a junction box below deck up through a gland and so to the fitting.

A simple type of gland can be made to suit any diameter of wire or group of wires. Each one should be wrapped with waterproof packing at the sleeve, then a further wrapping of packing is put round all the wires. Among suitable packing materials which are easy to obtain is Sylglas tape, a sticky, non-hardening, easily shaped, fabric-based tape used for glazing among other things. The flange should be bolted through the deck and the wires given a downward loop so that rain does not run down a long length of wire straight onto the gland.

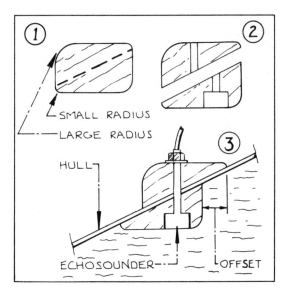

SMALL RADIUS
LARGE RADIUS
HULL
ECHOSOUNDER   OFFSET

Echosounder mount   To fit a transducer so that it is vertical, first round the edges of a block of wood, doing this while the block is still rectangular in section and therefore easy to grip in a vice. The next step is to drill out a large hole for the transducer head, allowing for swelling. The small hole for the stem of the transducer is not drilled at this stage as it should extend through a thick part of both chocks. The block is cut diagonally and the small hole for the stem is then drilled in the two parts. The fore and aft ends of the lower chock are well faired so that they do not disturb the water flow. The chocks are fitted on the inside and outside of the hull shell, with the inner one offset to give plenty of wood in way of the transducer stem on both sides.

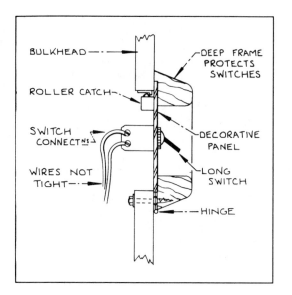

BULKHEAD ——·—

ROLLER CATCH ——·—

SWITCH
CONNECT<u>N</u>S ·

WIRES NOT
TIGHT ——·—

DEEP FRAME
PROTECTS
SWITCHES

DECORATIVE
PANEL

LONG
SWITCH

HINGE

Switch shield   An electric switch on a boat tends to suffer from corrosion and thus is not always the most reliable of fittings. If it is screwed into a panel which can be hinged out for inspection, annual cleaning will be quite simple. (This maintenance is the sort of job that can be done when weatherbound or when waiting for the tide.) It is important to leave some slack in the wires so that the panel can be hinged forward without snatching the wires out of the switch connections. By putting the hinge at the bottom no difficulty will be experienced working on the switch, whereas if the hinge was at the top an extra pair of hands would be needed. The deep frame round the switch is to prevent anyone falling against it and breaking or knocking it off accidentally.

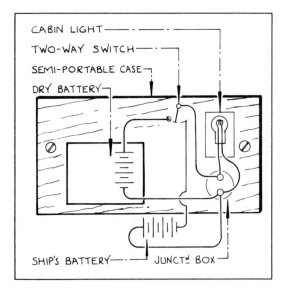

CABIN LIGHT ——·—·—

TWO-WAY SWITCH ——·—·

SEMI-PORTABLE CASE ¬

DRY BATTERY ¬

SHIP'S BATTERY ——·—   JUNCT<u>N</u> BOX

Standby lights   If there is one system and set of fittings which gives eternal trouble on small craft it is the lighting. Corrosion seems to be the main problem, but there are other worries such as failing batteries and defective switches. One way of by-passing most of these is to make up a cabin light on a semi-portable panel. At each laying-up time the panels are disconnected and taken ashore for overhaul. This particular panel has a two-way switch so that power can be taken from the ship's battery or the switch pushed across to the left and the dry battery used. The unit serves as an emergency light and can be used for both navigation and cabin lights.

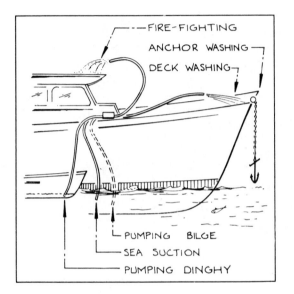

FIRE-FIGHTING

ANCHOR WASHING

DECK WASHING

PUMPING BILGE

SEA SUCTION

PUMPING DINGHY

Multi-purpose pump   A pump sited in a deck locker and driven by hand or its own motor can be a very versatile piece of equipment. It can be used to pump out the dinghy before lifting it aboard or to pump the bilges. It can suck up seawater to clean mud off the anchor chain or wash the decks. Also, it can be used to fight fire on board or on a neighbouring boat. This is an asset in these days of marinas : one burning boat in a marina may set fire to three others before the flames are put out.

It is important to get a pump which can easily lift the distance from the water to the deck. It may pay to site the pump lower down, since most can push water higher than the distance they can suck it up. The nozzle on the hose should be adjustable for delivering a spray or a jet.

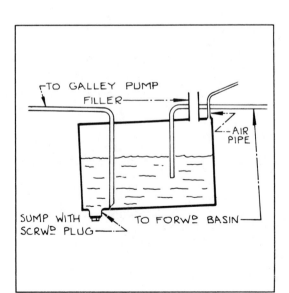

TO GALLEY PUMP

FILLER

AIR PIPE

SUMP WITH SCRW^D PLUG

TO FORW^D BASIN

Waterworks   This drawing outlines some of the features which make a successful fresh water plumbing system. There are two draw-off pipes, one to the basin forward, one to the galley. The former only extends two-thirds down the tank depth so anyone washing in the toilet compartment cannot use up all the water! The galley suction pipe has its end cut at 45° and pushed down into the tank until the tip touches the bottom ; the maker is thus sure that the pipe is as far down as possible. By drawing off through pipes which go through the top of the tank there is less risk of leaks where these pipes pass through the tank shell.

The installed tank is tilted, with the filler at the high end, as is the air vent pipe. The sump can be washed out by removing the plug.

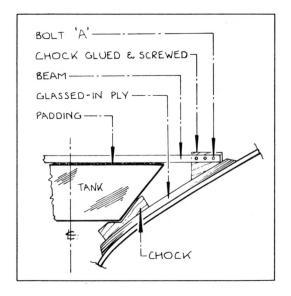

BOLT 'A'

CHOCK GLUED & SCREWED

BEAM

GLASSED-IN PLY

PADDING

TANK

CHOCK

Tight tanks Fitting a fuel or water tank into a hull so that there are no rattles can be difficult. It is important that a metal tank does not touch a fibreglass shell, otherwise the hull will be damaged at the point of contact.

One way of tackling the job is to glass in strips of thick plywood to the hull and to fit chocks to these to take the tank edges and its top securing beams. When fitting the beams, bolt A is put in first and the beam pivoted about this bolt. Padding is placed between the beam and the tank and the beam is knelt on while the other end is fastened. Additional fastenings can then be inserted at either end. The hull is protected and doubled in way of the load of the tank by the glassed-in strips of plywood.

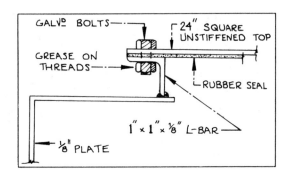

GALV⁰ BOLTS

24" SQUARE
UNSTIFFENED TOP

GREASE ON
THREADS

RUBBER SEAL

1" × 1" × ⅛" L-BAR

⅛" PLATE

Tank hatch The inside of a tank should be cleaned every winter and this unwelcome job can be made worse if the access hatch is small. Each hatch should be 2 × 2 ft so that a man can put his head and shoulders through. If the tank is made of $\frac{1}{8}$ in steel, then provided the hatch is on top it will not normally need any stiffening bars welded to it. It must have bolts all round spaced about 2 in apart. These bolts should be $\frac{5}{16}$ in diameter (for a tank of $\frac{1}{8}$ in steel) and if they are galvanized they will last as long as the tank. Lanolin on the threads will ensure that the nuts come off each year without a struggle. When making the rubber seal between the hatch and the angle-bar upstand the quickest way is to lay the hatch on the sheet of rubber and cut all round with a sharp, wetted knife. It is probably not worth cutting away the centre.

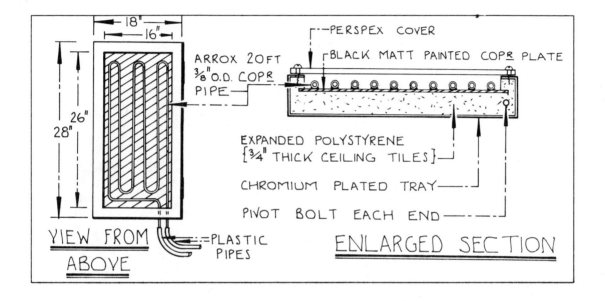

VIEW FROM ABOVE

18"
16"
26"
28"

ARROX 20FT ⅜" O.D. COPR PIPE

=PLASTIC PIPES

PERSPEX COVER

BLACK MATT PAINTED COPR PLATE

EXPANDED POLYSTYRENE {¾" THICK CEILING TILES}

CHROMIUM PLATED TRAY

PIVOT BOLT EACH END

ENLARGED SECTION

Water heater   A very simple solar water heater was designed and made by the owner of a Mediterranean-based yacht. A light copper tray was brazed up and chromium plated. In the bottom is a layer of expanded polystyrene ceiling tiles covered by a copper plate painted matt black. Brazed onto this is about 20 ft of ⅜ in o.d. copper pipe in zig-zags. Both inlet and outlet are in the same corner and join to flexible plastic tubing, so that when not in use the whole tray can be turned over and the polished bottom surface reflects instead of absorbing the sun's rays. The clear plastic (Perspex, Plexiglas or polycarbonate) prevents any breeze from cooling the water in the copper pipe, and this is most important wherever strong sun may be accompanied by a cooling breeze. Heat penetrates the plastic and is absorbed by the black-painted copper. Water is pushed through the heater by a centrifugal pump which uses very little power, particularly when flow is restricted by a cock. In fact so little power is needed that a wind-driven pump might be used, or a gravity feed.

Trials in mid-March at 10.30 a.m. when the sky was almost clear gave a temperature rise from 58° to 102°F with a flow rate of 1 pint in 5 minutes. In midsummer the heating rate would be much better. Once heated, the water has to be kept in an insulated container.

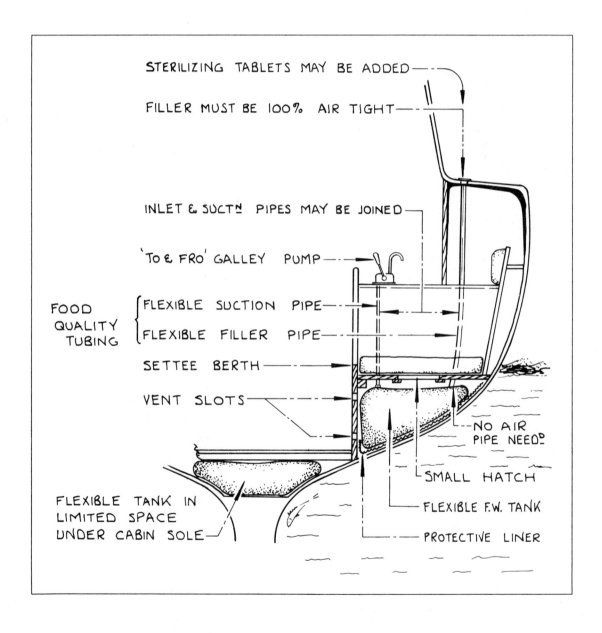

STERILIZING TABLETS MAY BE ADDED

FILLER MUST BE 100% AIR TIGHT

INLET & SUCT^N PIPES MAY BE JOINED

'TO & FRO' GALLEY PUMP

FOOD QUALITY TUBING
{
FLEXIBLE SUCTION PIPE
FLEXIBLE FILLER PIPE

SETTEE BERTH

VENT SLOTS

NO AIR PIPE NEED^D

SMALL HATCH

FLEXIBLE TANK IN LIMITED SPACE UNDER CABIN SOLE

FLEXIBLE F.W. TANK

PROTECTIVE LINER

Flexible water tanks   A practical way of
increasing a yacht's tank capacity, flexible
tanks take advantage of odd available spaces and
can be installed through relatively small hatches
and awkward access openings without requiring
the dismantling of joinery. Metal tanks under
the berths tend to gurgle as the boat moves,
whereas the flexible type makes little or no
noise even during quite severe motion.

A flexible tank does not need an air vent pipe
(which usefully saves fitting time and expense)
because as water is pumped out the top of the
tank collapses. However the filler pipe must
have a completely airtight cap to prevent seawater getting in and for effective suction. If
the filler and suction pipes are joined to a single
lead into the tank it is even more important to
have an airtight filler cap. All the piping can
be flexible plastic tubing, and for fresh water
systems (shown here) it should be 'food quality'
plastic, which sometimes has a purple tinge.
It is sold by firms which supply pubs, breweries,
bars and caterers.

Water tanks should be cleaned out about four
times a year using a weak detergent solution
(not a biological detergent) for the first rinse and
ordinary fresh water for the three subsequent
rinses. It may pay to remove the whole unit for
internal and external washing.

There should be a protective liner (such as a
piece of $\frac{1}{2}$ in foam plastic) between tank and
hull to prevent wear. It is imperative that there
are no screws or nails through the furniture
which may penetrate the tank, or splinters, or
rough edges of fibreglass. Ventilation slots
prevent a buildup of moisture and mildew.

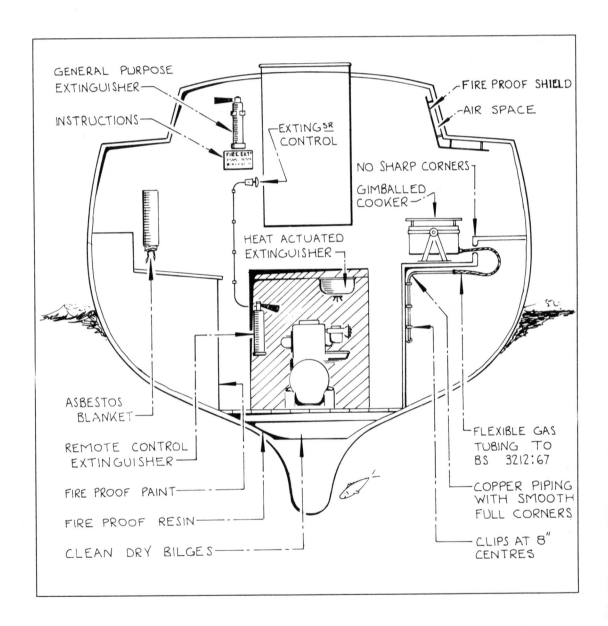

Fireproofing   The worst place to put a fire
extinguisher is near a galley stove, because if
the stove bursts into flames no one will be
able to reach the extinguisher. A position by
the companionway is handy to anyone on deck
or below. It is no bad idea to have the operating
instructions written out and mounted on a bulkhead where everyone will read them at intervals
before the blaze is going fiercely.

An asbestos blanket is also good for putting
out galley fires or wrapping around a person
whose clothes are burning, but it should be
stowed well away from hatches and the
companionway since it tends to blot up water.

In the engine compartment an automatic fire
extinguishing system is a good idea, but cannot
always be relied upon because sometimes the
fire starts just out of range of the sensing unit
and burns for some time before the actuator
reaches a high enough temperature to operate.
Additional sensors and a second remote-
controlled extinguisher should be fitted in the
engine area so that crew on deck or below can
operate it as soon as a fire is noticed.

Bilges should be kept clean and dry so that
oil and fuel spillage is seen at once and cleaned
up. Muck and shavings in the bilge have a bad
habit of soaking up fuel and becoming an
added hazard, as well as blocking pumps.

A gimballed gas stove must have a flexible
connecting hose made to BS 3212:67 or the
equivalent local specifications. It has to be kept
clear of all sharp corners and edges on the
furniture, stove or hull, and long enough to
allow the stove to swing freely but otherwise
kept to a minimum length. If possible copper
piping should be in one continuous length
from the gas bottle to the flexible connection.

To protect the yacht the structure above the
stove should be fitted with a fireproof shield to
prevent charring and delay the effects of any
outbreak of fire. The air gap between the shield
and the hull should be as big as possible, and
certainly not less than $\frac{3}{4}$ in, with $1\frac{1}{2}$ in a much
better minimum distance.

Joinery

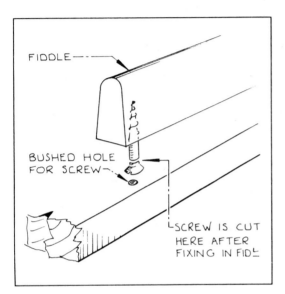

FIDDLE

BUSHED HOLE
FOR SCREW

SCREW IS CUT
HERE AFTER
FIXING IN FIDᴸ

Free fiddle   For a boat which is not
engaged in serious deep sea work there is a
lot to be said for a fiddle which is relatively
light and can be removed. A simple way to make
a portable fiddle is to use ordinary brass screws
as pegs. The screws are driven upwards into
the fiddle and their heads chopped off. The
fiddle is next put in place on the table top and
pushed down so that each decapitated screw
leaves a little mark. This mark is then used for
drilling and the hole is bushed with brass or
copper. The screw end should project $\frac{3}{4}$ in or
more into the table top and the spacing should
not be much more than 8 in.

  A more subtle shape of fixed fiddle is shown
below; it blends well with surrounding joinery
and also serves as a drawer pull.

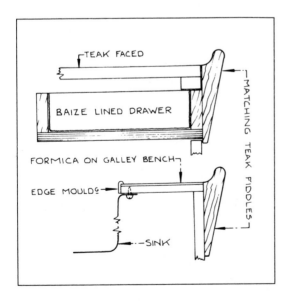

TEAK FACED

MATCHING TEAK FIDDLES

BAIZE LINED DRAWER

FORMICA ON GALLEY BENCH

EDGE MOULDS

SINK

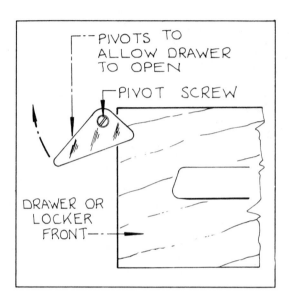

PIVOTS TO ALLOW DRAWER TO OPEN

PIVOT SCREW

DRAWER OR LOCKER FRONT

Gravity turnbutton   No one wants drawers or lockers to burst open as soon as the weather gets rough. This simple turnbutton has the advantage of being easy and cheap to make: it is simply a triangle of metal, hardwood, $\frac{1}{4}$ in Perspex or other clear plastic or Tufnol pivoted loosely so it hangs in a locking position. The pivot screw and button must be strong enough to take the full weight of the drawer or locker and its contents, which may be tins of food or heavy tools. The drawer should not be fitted with more than one button since it would be difficult to hold them aside to release the drawer.

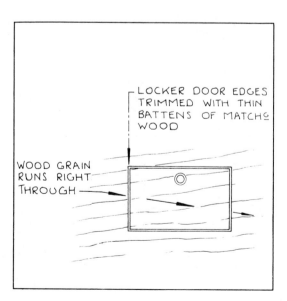

LOCKER DOOR EDGES TRIMMED WITH THIN BATTENS OF MATCHG WOOD

WOOD GRAIN RUNS RIGHT THROUGH

Matched grain   All the wooden doors are cut from the panels in which they are to be so that the grain is uninterrupted on all furniture facings. The saw cut is filled by a narrow wood trim round each locker door giving a most attractive finish, and incidentally a lightweight type of furniture.

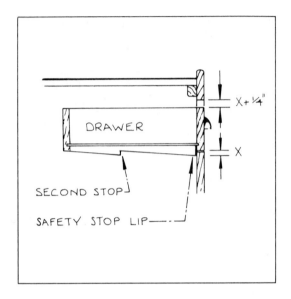

Secure drawer   A lip on the runner which engages on the drawer front lower facing is commonly used to stop drawers sliding open. An improvement is a second lip near the back of the drawer so that it is impossible to pull it all the way out accidentally. It also acts as a long-stop against the front one failing, as happens occasionally. The two lips are usually about $\frac{3}{8}$ in deep and then the gap above the closed drawer is about $\frac{5}{8}$ in. It is important that the space, shown as $X + \frac{1}{4}$ in in the sketch, is clearly bigger than the safety lip or the drawer may jam.

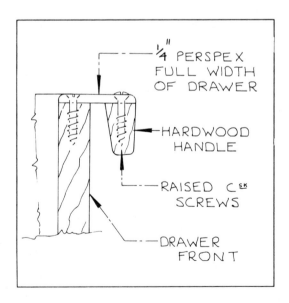

Drawer handle   This handle can be used for a cupboard as well, set vertically down the opening edge. The strip across the top does not have to be of Perspex (Lucite) ; it can be aluminium, Tufnol or a strong plastic. It should not be thinner than $\frac{1}{4}$ in if plastic, and should extend the full width of the drawer for adequate strength. Both top edges are rounded. The handle should be screwed to the strip with at least 1 in screws at about 3 in centres. If the drawer front is too thin to take the screws it may be necessary to glue and screw a thickening piece along the top to give sufficient width. Raised countersunk screws in the handle improve appearance.

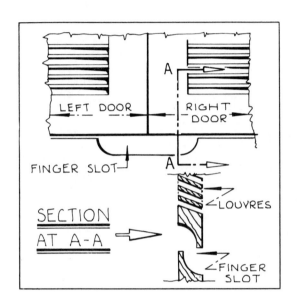

Louvred doors   Fully louvred panels assist the continual ventilation of closed compartments. No handles are needed, which gives a clean and attractive appearance. To open the door it is only necessary to slip the fingers into a wide slot grooved in the door under the thicker bottom slat.

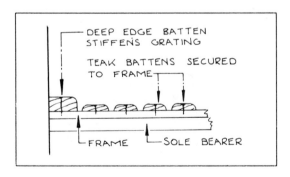

Batten sole   Oiled teak can be used like this for the sole in the toilet compartment. Each batten is rounded and there are gaps between the battens to help air circulation and promote drying out.

The battens are held in a frame which lifts out in one piece. This is convenient for cleaning and laying up. The frame rests on bearers around the periphery of the compartment and the whole grating can be made up away from the boat. It is usually made to a jig, so that it fits exactly, neatly and securely. The battens are quite thin to save weight and because teak is costly. To give the grating adequate strength the edge battens are thick, but like the middle ones, their edges are well rounded.

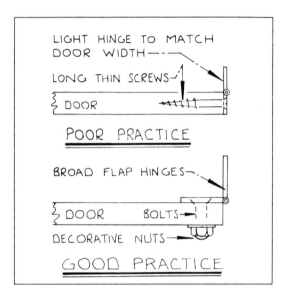

Door flaw   Some doors on small yachts are of light $\frac{1}{2}$ in or $\frac{5}{8}$ in ply. It is possible to buy hinges with flaps only $\frac{1}{2}$ in wide and screw these into the edge of the door, but in practice this type of hinge does not last more than one or two seasons because it is too light for normal yachting use and its fastenings are unreliable in such thin material.

There is nothing like a set of bolts secured right through the door panels. Much better, have a slightly chunky-looking hinge which will hold even when somebody falls heavily against the door, rather than a flimsy, if more elegant, fitting.

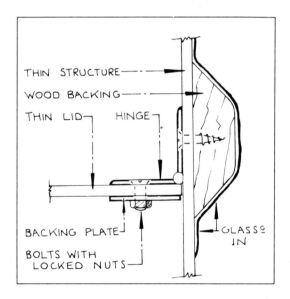

Securing hinges   Many yachts by the end of their third hard season, or even before, have a number of locker lids torn off. Light doors are found to have loose hinge screws and even some moderately heavy hatches are found to be coming adrift. All these troubles stem from the same basic engineering weakness in the join of the hinges to the structure and to the moving part. Unless there is ample 'meat' a wood screw cannot have enough grip. If it is replaced by a bolt, the nuts may pull through unless there is a full backing plate. Ordinary washers tend to be too small, but a backing plate the same size as the hinge leaf works for a lifetime. Where screws have to be used (when there is no access for putting on nuts) an added backing piece of ample thickness and length is essential.

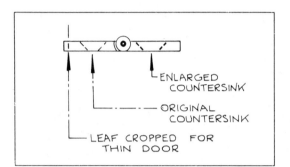

Nylon hinges   For the owner who wants to save weight, the search for light equipment must extend to every part of the yacht. Nylon hinges are lighter than metal ones, and though the saving on one pair is small it can add up if there are many lockers and doors. A count on one 41 ft motorsailer, where admittedly weight was not important, showed that there were forty hinges aboard.

Another advantage of nylon hinges is the ease with which the countersink for the screws can be enlarged if big screws are necessary. The leaves can be trimmed to fit exactly. This can be done with brass hinges, but not so easily.

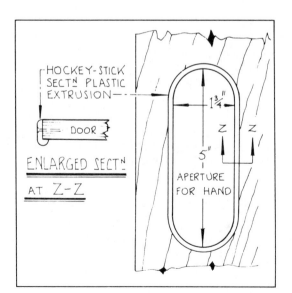

Hole handle   Some doors do not shut off an area which requires privacy; for instance the door to an oilskin locker may have an aperture cut through it, but the same cannot be said of the toilet compartment. The door 'handle' shown is suitable where privacy is not required.

It is made by cutting a slot big enough to take an adult's hand. The hole must be cut back $1\frac{1}{2}$ in from the edge of the door, possibly even 2–3 in, for strength and also to give a landing for the fingers. The edge of the wood is covered with a suitable aluminium or plastic moulding. One type is the flexible 'hockey stick' section illustrated. It should be nailed at close intervals and each nail should be punched in.

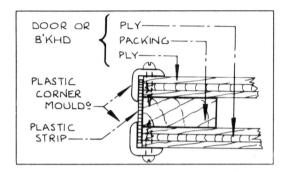

Thick bulkhead edging   The majority of fibreglass yachts, in fact most yachts whatever the hull material, now have ply bulkheads. The doorways through are cut out and edged with plastic strip. This strip moulding comes in various sizes and colours, but it is only available for fairly thin bulkheads.

When a double bulkhead is made, perhaps to help support a mast or a pair of heavy engines, or for soundproofing, none of the standard mouldings is wide enough. To circumvent the difficulty corner mouldings which have an L-section are used each side to keep in place a flat strip of plastic or wood veneer. This strip can be cut from a wide sheet, and its edges do not have to be neat or fair because they are not exposed.

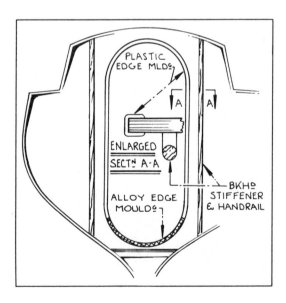

Bulkhead doorway   All sorts of craft made of various materials have strength bulkheads. The doorways through such panels must be cut with well rounded ends, to avoid potential weak areas at the corners. Where the bulkhead is thin, and most are thin in order to save weight and money, some sort of stiffening is needed. It is no bad idea to make virtue out of necessity and scallop the stiffeners so that they form hand grips. The hand slots must not be too long and there must be bolts close above and below each one, otherwise the stiffeners will not live up to their name.

The edge of the doorway needs some sort of cover, especially if ply is used. There is now available a range of plastic extrusions to encase the edges of all thicknesses of ply.

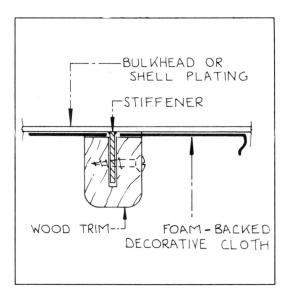

BULKHEAD OR
SHELL PLATING

STIFFENER

WOOD TRIM

FOAM-BACKED
DECORATIVE CLOTH

Lining A quick and rather smart method of covering a steel bulkhead is shown here. The same technique can also be used on the inside of shell plating, or inside a cabin top.

A leathercloth with a thin skin of foam on the back is glued to the steel. The edges are brought near but not right up against the stiffener and then a simple wood trim piece is rabetted with a circular saw and pushed in place, to be secured at wide intervals by a screw through the steel. The cloth does not need to be fitted accurately right up to the stiffener and the whole job is quick, calls for little skill and yet gives an attractive appearance.

The technique can also be used where the stiffeners are angle-bars, and a bevelled wood strip will finish the edge neatly.

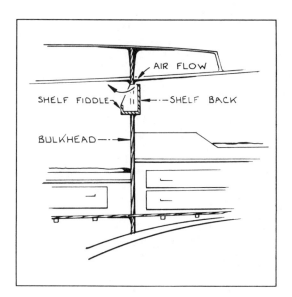

AIR FLOW

SHELF FIDDLE

SHELF BACK

BULKHEAD

Book-rack vent A fault in many production yachts is that they lack access for air to flow through the hull. As most of these boats are built to a strictly competitive price, items which do not catch the eye at a boat show are omitted. Because ventilation is one way to reduce smells, as well as condensation, holes in every bulkhead, locker front and panel have a valuable effect.

This bookshelf is recessed into the forward bulkhead of the saloon so that it is unobtrusive, yet it does not take up useful space in the fore cabin. There is no top on it, so air goes over the top of the books. The fiddle on the aft edge should be only about $1\frac{1}{2}$ in high, otherwise it will be difficult to get books into the shelf. Books should not fall out provided the shelf is arranged athwartships.

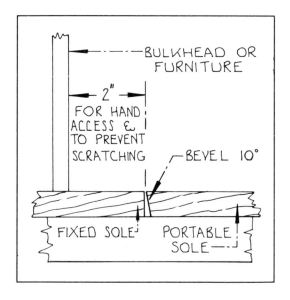

Freeing floorboards   From dinghy to gin palace, cabin and cockpit floorboards tend to jam as they swell with water. A simple solution is to bevel the edges of the boards by about 10°. Even if the top edge still binds all that is needed is a slight jerk. The edges of the portable boards should be well clear of bulkheads and furniture, to allow a hand to be inserted underneath and avoid scratching the joinery.

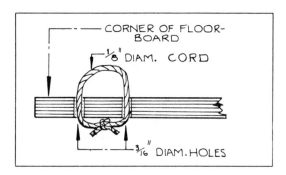

Floorboard lifter   Any yachtsman who has had more than two weeks' experience knows the curse of jammed floorboards. This is a universal plague, found in power and sailing yachts, in 2-tonners and 200-tonners. It can be dangerous if the seized floorboard is over a leak or an overheating piece of machinery.

One cheap way to make floorboards liftable is to drill a 1 in diameter finger hole at each end. However this is not totally satisfactory, since it does not permit a really good grip. Just as cheap but many times more effective is the trick sketched here. The synthetic line is tough and is set in a little from the edge of the board so that when considerable force is applied, the board does not break. A large screwdriver or bar can be slipped under the loop so that if need be two people can heave on the board.

The other part of the remedy is to trim the board edges slightly, as shown above.

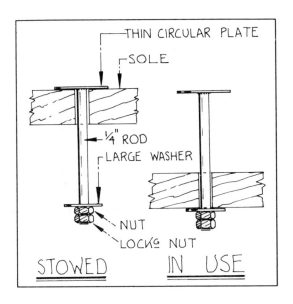

THIN CIRCULAR PLATE

SOLE

$\frac{1}{4}$" ROD

LARGE WASHER

NUT

LOCKᴳ NUT

STOWED   IN USE

Sole lifter   When stowed, this device is almost flush with the sole since the top plate is only $\frac{1}{16}$ in thick. Its diameter is $1\frac{1}{2}$ in and it is welded to the $\frac{1}{4}$ in rod which fits in a $\frac{3}{8}$ in hole through the sole. On the bottom there is a large washer, a nut and locking nut. The top plate is lifted up so that the fingers can then get a good grip on the rod.

For heavy engine covering hatches the whole fitting can be reproduced in a larger size so that two hands can grip a $\frac{1}{2}$ in rod. Fabrication and fitting is cheap and quick, and with no moving parts little can go wrong.

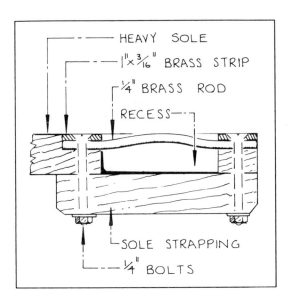

HEAVY SOLE

1"×$\frac{3}{16}$" BRASS STRIP

$\frac{1}{4}$" BRASS ROD

RECESS

SOLE STRAPPING

$\frac{1}{4}$" BOLTS

Heavy handle   The cabin sole above the engine compartment is often massive, to take plenty of weight and for soundproofing. Unfortunately this type of heavy panel needs a very rugged lifting handle large enough to give a good grip, and these are not easy to find. Those available are sometimes made of steel, and rust, and many have flimsy fastenings.

A made-up handle is shown, using easily available components. The brass straps must have two bolts each end. The rod need not be brazed to the straps but merely lodged beneath them. It may be necessary to gouge out the sole strapping since there must be about $1\frac{3}{4}$ in of space below the rod for a man's hand.

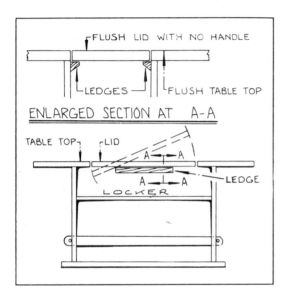

FLUSH LID WITH NO HANDLE

LEDGES

FLUSH TABLE TOP

ENLARGED SECTION AT A-A

TABLE TOP

LID

A — A

A — A

LEDGE

LOCKER

Hidden locker   This idea goes back a great many years and for quite a long time was apparently forgotten by designers and builders. It consists of nothing more than a locker with a flush lid in a saloon table. Any handle on the locker would interrupt the smooth appearance of the table top and also cause small objects like cruets to tip over if they were set on the handle. The lid consists of a flat piece of wood lying flush with the top and sitting on two ledges. The ledges do not extend quite the full length of the lid so that by depressing one end of it the other tips up. The dotted line shows the lid tipped prior to being lifted off. This ingenious device requires no bought-in fittings.

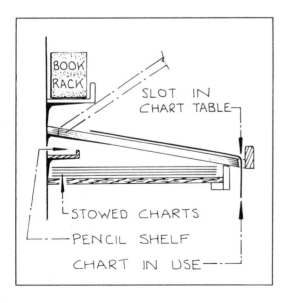

BOOK RACK

SLOT IN CHART TABLE

STOWED CHARTS

PENCIL SHELF

CHART IN USE

Tuck-down chart   A slot along the lower edge of a chart table enables the chart to be slipped through and passed vertically down so that the relevant part of the chart can be drawn towards the navigator. This arrangement is particularly useful if there is not space for a chart table with the full north-south dimensions of a standard chart. The upper edge of the slot must be well rounded to prevent the chart becoming creased and to help ease it through the slot. If there is a book rack at the head of the chart table it must be high enough to allow the table top to hinge up and give access to the locker.

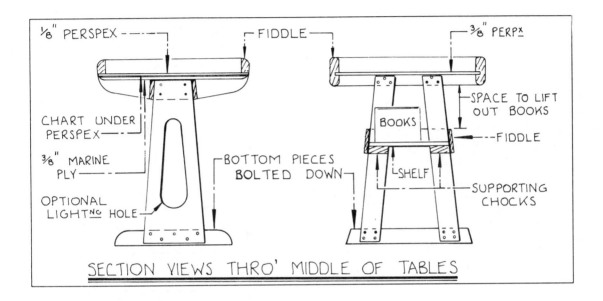

1/8" PERSPEX — FIDDLE — 3/8" PERPᵪ

CHART UNDER PERSPEX

3/8" MARINE PLY

OPTIONAL LIGHTᴺᴳ HOLE

BOTTOM PIECES BOLTED DOWN

BOOKS

SPACE TO LIFT OUT BOOKS

FIDDLE

SHELF

SUPPORTING CHOCKS

SECTION VIEWS THRO' MIDDLE OF TABLES

Tables   Cabin tables tend to be monotonously similar. For a change two alternative designs are suggested here. On the left the table top is made up of Perspex, Plexiglas or polycarbonate on marine ply with a chart sandwiched between. The fiddles all round should be higher than the rims of the yacht's deepest plates. The end fiddles are bolted to the legs which are in turn bolted to the bottom pieces.

On the right hand side is the same basic idea, but with a bookshelf underneath. The titles of the books can be seen by looking down through the table top. In each case glass might be substituted for plastic, but it should of course be one of the unbreakable types. There must be some form of stiffening to prevent the tables distorting in a fore-and-aft plane : on the left this takes the form of vertical pieces either side at the tops of the legs. One the right the fiddles either side of the bookcase provide a useful measure of

stiffness. They and the fastenings to the cabin sole must withstand the weight of a heavy man falling against the table.

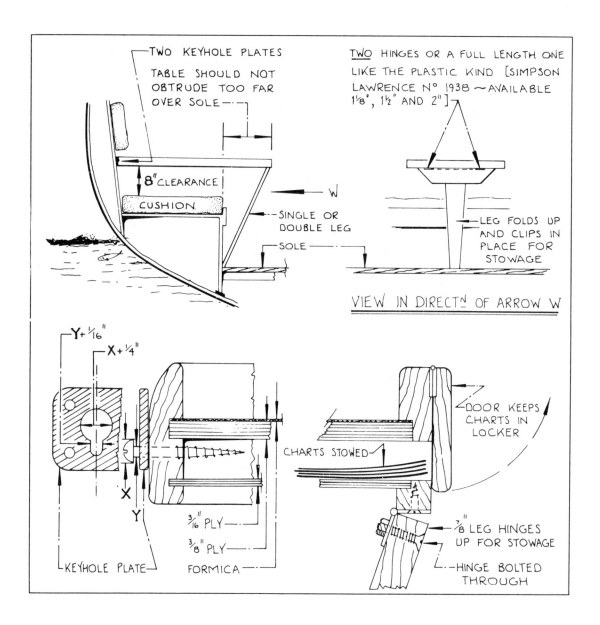

TWO KEYHOLE PLATES

TABLE SHOULD NOT OBTRUDE TOO FAR OVER SOLE

8" CLEARANCE

CUSHION

SINGLE OR DOUBLE LEG

SOLE

W

TWO HINGES OR A FULL LENGTH ONE LIKE THE PLASTIC KIND [SIMPSON LAWRENCE N° 1938 ~ AVAILABLE 1⅛", 1½" AND 2"]

LEG FOLDS UP AND CLIPS IN PLACE FOR STOWAGE

VIEW IN DIRECTⁿ OF ARROW W

Y + 1/16"

X + ¼"

X

Y

KEYHOLE PLATE

3/16" PLY

3/8" PLY

FORMICA

CHARTS STOWED

DOOR KEEPS CHARTS IN LOCKER

⅞ LEG HINGES UP FOR STOWAGE

HINGE BOLTED THROUGH

Cabin table and chart store   The sketches
show details of a portable table which can be
used for meals or chartwork. One can be made
for each side of the cabin. Top left is the section
view from forward or aft through each side of the
saloon, and top right is a view looking outboard.
Bottom left is an enlarged section through the
outboard edge of the cabin table showing
how it is suspended from two keyhole plates.
Bottom right is an enlarged section through the
inboard edge and access to the chart stowage
space.

The structure is in the form of a shallow box
made up of an upper layer of $\frac{3}{8}$ in ply and a
bottom of $\frac{3}{16}$ in ply. The gap between will be
about $1-2\frac{1}{2}$ in deep, and this is where the
charts are stowed. The top of the table forms
the working surface; fiddles all round form the
sides and end of the chart locker.

Outboard the table rests in and is held firmly
at the corners by two keyhole plates, which are
easily made from $\frac{1}{4}$ in or even $\frac{1}{2}$ in brass. They
may be chromed after all the holes have been
drilled and filed. Large round-headed screws
engage in the plates, their screws being driven
through the ends of the fore-and-aft outboard
fiddles and on into the athwartships fiddles, to
give a good grip. Alternatively, bolts through the
outboard section of the fiddle could be used.

The table should be set 8 in above the cushion
to give kneeroom, and it should not project out
into the cabin so far as to make moving past
difficult.

Interior

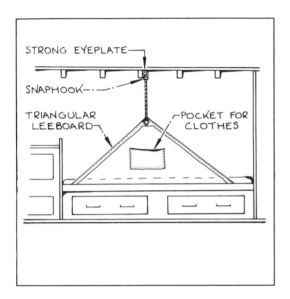

STRONG EYEPLATE
SNAPHOOK
TRIANGULAR LEEBOARD
POCKET FOR CLOTHES

Light leeboard This pattern of leeboard has only one lashing which in turn needs only one eyeplate (not a screweye). It must be triangular in shape if it has a single rope, but it is effective in keeping the sleeper in provided there is support for his shoulders, thighs and knees, and is ideal for children. The pocket is for clothes which are taken off before turning in. If the fabric is cotton canvas it will be cheaper than a synthetic fibre cloth, but it is likely to hold moisture longer when it gets damp unless dressed with a water-repellant preservative.

LEEBOARD IN USE
LEEBOARD STOWED
QUARTER BERTH LOOKS INBOARD

Daggerboard leeboard Looking towards the centreline of a yacht from the port quarter berth, the sketch shows a type of leeboard which is always ready for immediate use, yet concealed when not required. There are no ropes, no hooks to clip into eyes, nothing which is awkward to do when the boat is pounding along with her cabin coamings under.

The leeboard is a long plank with a flat handle at the forward end and is housed in a casing at the bottom of the berth, like a dagger in its sheath. The board laps below the berth coaming and is supported by it. When fully extended there are still several inches of the leeboard in the casing. A barrel bolt at the forward end may be necessary, but with careful proportioning should not be needed since the board gains its main support from the berth coaming.

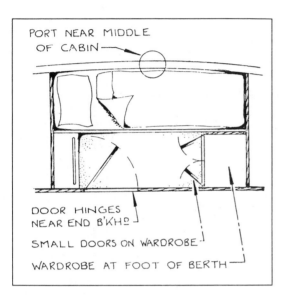

PORT NEAR MIDDLE OF CABIN

DOOR HINGES NEAR END B'KH?

SMALL DOORS ON WARDROBE

WARDROBE AT FOOT OF BERTH

Cabin comfort   Some basic principles for a comfortable single cabin can be seen here. The porthole is near the middle of the cabin for maximum light and a feeling of space. The door is set so as to open into the cabin in such a way that one steps into the middle of the space. This is opposite to house building practice, where doors are often hinged on the side away from the adjacent wall. To avoid cluttering the floor space there are two narrow doors on the wardrobe; a single one would sweep too much area and make access awkward. The wardrobe is at the foot of the berth rather than the head so the dressing table can double as a bedside table. Also, if the wardrobe was at the head of the berth, the sleeper would have his head in what would seem like a tunnel between the tall locker and the ship's side.

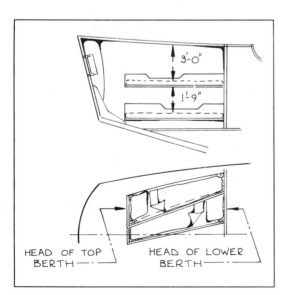

3'-0"

1'-9"

HEAD OF TOP BERTH

HEAD OF LOWER BERTH

Berth juxtaposition   In a 48 ft ketch with a poop deck the owner wanted upper and lower berths. There was not enough height to give the required 3 ft sitting-up headroom over both berths, as the lower berth could not be right down on the sole due to the shape of the hull.

By reversing the top berth, so that its head was over the foot of the lower one, and bringing the lower berth inboard, adequate headroom was found. The lower berth is tucked slightly under the upper, but not so much that anyone in the lower berth would find it uncomfortable to sit up. This arrangement is not practical without permanent leeboards, because at the narrow foot of the berths the bedding will come off to easily unless there is some sort of surround.

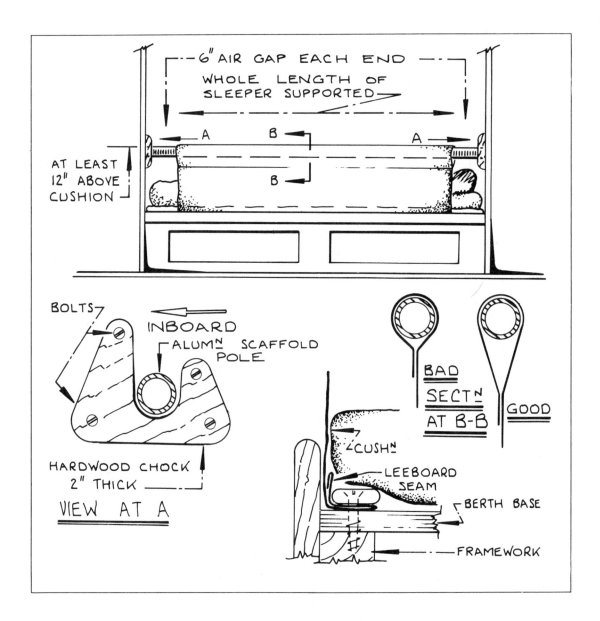

6" AIR GAP EACH END

WHOLE LENGTH OF
SLEEPER SUPPORTED

A   B   A

B

AT LEAST
12" ABOVE
CUSHION

BOLTS

INBOARD

ALUMᴺ SCAFFOLD
POLE

HARDWOOD CHOCK
2" THICK

VIEW AT A

BAD

SECTᴺ

AT B-B   GOOD

CUSHᴺ

LEEBOARD
SEAM

BERTH BASE

FRAMEWORK

Strong leeboard   A really rugged leeboard
which can stand up to the worst weather is
shown in these sketches. The tube is either a
standard hollow steel or aluminium scaffold pole
or a 1 in steel pipe. It slides through the hem
in the canvas leeboard and drops into wooden
or metal chocks, shown bottom left. It will be
seen that the two horns are of different heights:
the inboard one is made too high for the tube
inside the leeboard to lift over whereas the
outboard one is just low enough for the tube
to be forced over the top.

The upper hem in the leeboard should be a
wide one, not only to make it easy to slide the
tube through but also to lessen the tension on
the stitching. If the overlap is quite small there
will be a tendency for the stitching to be forced
apart. The bottom edge is secured by a wooden
or Tufnol batten screwed at about $2\frac{1}{2}$ in centres.
Round-headed screws with washers can be
used instead, but these tend to tear out eventually, particularly at the ends of the fabric, when
severely tested.

The leeboard will probably be made of 10 oz
Terylene (Dacron) or 12 oz proofed cotton
canvas. As shown it is strong enough to sit on
or fall against, and it should keep the sleeper
and his bedding in regardless of the weather.
It also keeps out a lot of light, which helps
sleeping in the daytime.

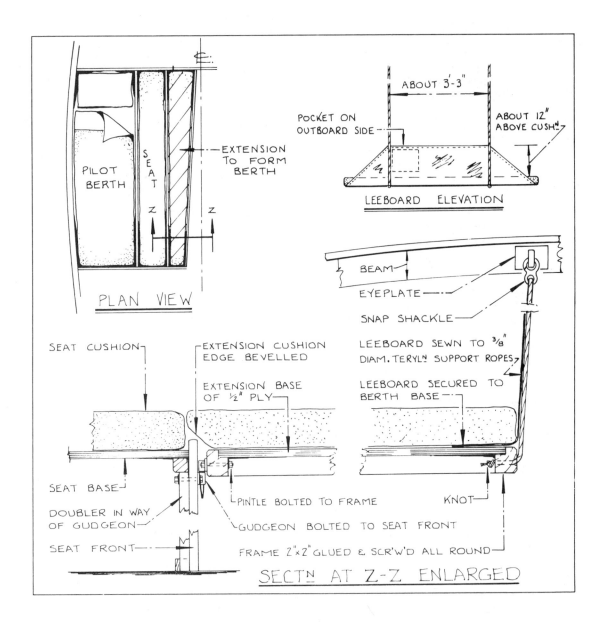

PLAN VIEW

PILOT
BERTH

S
E
A
T

Z   Z

EXTENSION
TO FORM
BERTH

LEEBOARD   ELEVATION

ABOUT 3'-3"

POCKET ON
OUTBOARD SIDE

ABOUT 12"
ABOVE CUSHⁿ

BEAM

EYEPLATE

SNAP SHACKLE

LEEBOARD SEWN TO ³/₈"
DIAM. TERYLⁿ SUPPORT ROPES

LEEBOARD SECURED TO
BERTH BASE

SEAT CUSHION

EXTENSION CUSHION
EDGE BEVELLED

EXTENSION BASE
OF ½" PLY

SEAT BASE

DOUBLER IN WAY
OF GUDGEON

SEAT FRONT

PINTLE BOLTED TO FRAME

GUDGEON BOLTED TO SEAT FRONT

FRAME 2"x2" GLUED & SCR'W'D ALL ROUND

KNOT

SECTⁿ AT Z-Z ENLARGED

An extra berth   On yachts which have
outboard pilot berths there is often a long narrow
seat adjacent in the saloon. Various ingenious
ways of making this seat into a spare berth
have been devised, and the sketches show one
of the simplest and least expensive. The extension needs to be the same width down its full
length. If, when the extension is in place, the
cabin sole area will be restricted, it may pay
to keep the foot end quite narrow. As a general
rule, the complete bunk should be at least
1 ft 9 in wide at the shoulders and 14 in at the
foot.

   The extension shown consists of a plywood
base on a strong wood frame. The outboard
edge has a pair of ordinary, strong dinghy
rudder pintles which drop into gudgeons
on the seat front; the inboard side is supported
by a pair of non-stretching ropes, or possibly
three. The ropes also support the leeboard, an
addition which is required even if this berth is
not used at sea. The cushion on the extension
should be the same thickness as the seat cushion
and 3 in is a good working minimum, with 4 in
where real comfort is sought. It will probably pay
to secure the extention cushion to the base. The
pocket in the leeboard is for stowing clothes
when sleeping. The ropes supporting the berth
and leeboard are snap-shackled to eyeplates in
the beam above the berth. If an eyeplate is not
praticable an adequately fixed eyebolt could
be used, though this does not spread the load
as well. (Eyeplates and eyebolts are discussed
elsewhere in this book.)

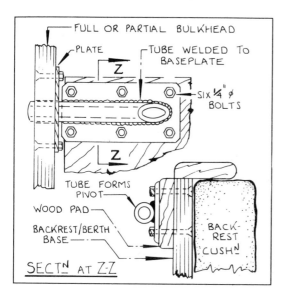

FULL OR PARTIAL BULKHEAD

PLATE

TUBE WELDED TO BASEPLATE

Z

SIX ¼" ⌀ BOLTS

Z

TUBE FORMS PIVOT

WOOD PAD

BACKREST/BERTH BASE

BACK-REST CUSHⁿ

SECTⁿ AT Z-Z

Berth hinges   When a settee back is used to form an upper berth the hinges must each be strong enough to support the weight of a man. It is not enough to have the hinges just adequate to carry the weight between them since by sitting on one end of the berth all the weight comes on a single hinge. It is not easy to get really strong hinges and this pivot has many advantages over the normal type. Precise alignment is not necessary; provided the hole in the bulkhead which takes the pivot is slightly oversize, up to 10° misalignment is not serious.
The pivot is made of tube, approximately $\frac{3}{4}$ in in diameter or even bigger. It should not be less than $\frac{3}{4}$ in and should be at least 8 in long so that there can be plenty of fastenings.

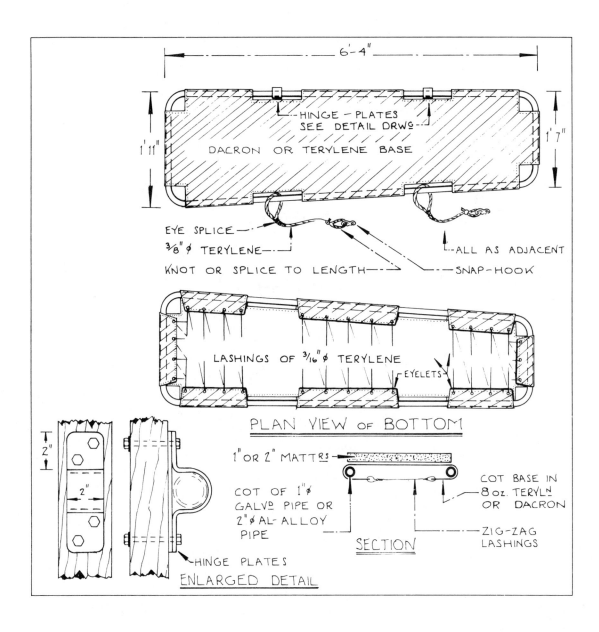

6'-4"

HINGE - PLATES
SEE DETAIL DRWG

DACRON OR TERYLENE BASE

1'11"

1'7"

EYE SPLICE
3/8"⌀ TERYLENE

ALL AS ADJACENT

KNOT OR SPLICE TO LENGTH

SNAP-HOOK

LASHINGS OF 3/16"⌀ TERYLENE

EYELETS

PLAN VIEW of BOTTOM

2"

2"

1" OR 2" MATT'RS

COT OF 1"⌀
GALV'D PIPE OR
2"⌀ AL-ALLOY
PIPE

COT BASE IN
8 oz. TERYL'N
OR DACRON

ZIG-ZAG
LASHINGS

SECTION

HINGE PLATES

ENLARGED DETAIL

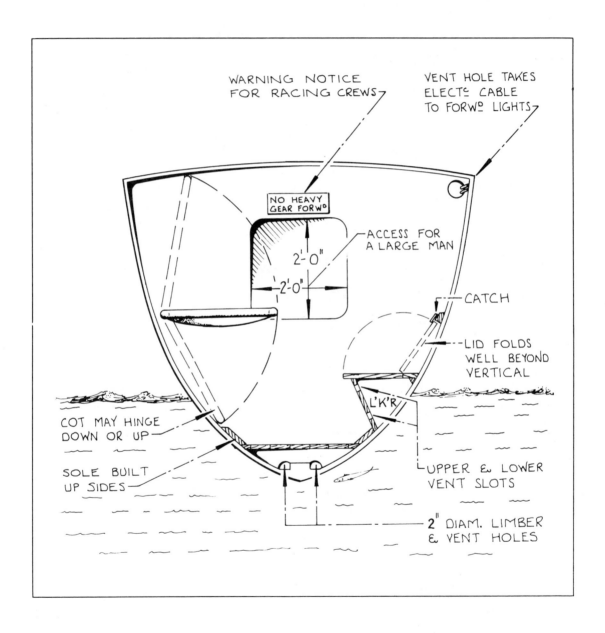

Space planning   Nothing heavy should be
stored in the bow of any seagoing boat, whether
power or sail. It is not a bad thing to have a
warning notice discouraging people from dump-
ing spare anchors out of sight forward of the bow
bulkhead. At the same time the forepeak should
be accessible, so any apertures through the
bulkhead should be big enough for a heavy man
to crawl through. Ventilation is very important in
these end spaces, and it is not enough to have
one hole since air requires an inlet and outlet to
circulate. To this end there is a large vent hole
at one corner of the bulkhead and also limber
holes big enough to act as vent holes down at
the bottom. Since wet sails are likely to be
dumped in fo'c's'le lockers pairs of vent holes
are particularly necessary otherwise the moisture
never escapes and mildew will grow. Locker lids
should fold well back beyond the vertical and
have catches to ensure that they stay open, so
both hands can be used to rummage in the
locker even when the boat is heeled.

It is usual to stow pipe cots upwards, but it
can be much more convenient to let them drop
down; it is not always easy to arrange for a
securing button at the deckhead to keep the
cot up. Incidentally, the cot can be allowed to
obtrude across the access hole in the forward
bulkhead without causing much inconvenience.

The cabin sole is shown carried up each side,
for convenience when the boat is heeled and
to prevent scuff marks.

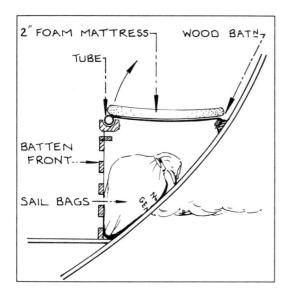

2" FOAM MATTRESS⌐   WOOD BAT⊼₇

TUBE⌐

BATTEN
FRONT⋯

SAIL BAGS →

Sail store   If there is one thing that hard-working crews loathe it is a stowage place which is cramped. If sailbags have to be forced through small locker doors, then sail changes will tend to be put off, especially if the crew are feeling a bit seasick.

Sails can be stowed under the two berths in the fo'c's'le. Access could not be better, since the whole berth base lifts up. The outboard side of the berth base (which is of woven synthetic material) is screwed through a wood batten into a stringer in the hull moulding. The inboard side is made into a pocket to hold an aluminium tube which rests in two wood chocks.

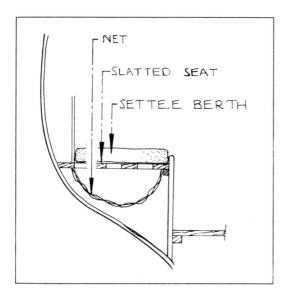

⌐ NET

⌐SLATTED SEAT

⌐SETTEE BERTH

Net gain   The space beneath settees in a modern yacht is sometimes sealed off. The front is bonded to the hull and at each end there are bulkheads or other solid divisions. As a result anything stowed underneath is subject to damp and mildew.

To cure this problem, holes should be cut in the end bulkheads, the settee fronts, or both. However that is not the whole story. Bilgewater can slop up the side, condensation forms against the hull's inner surface, and so on. So for stowage it is a good idea to suspend netting under the settee base. If it is made of a synthetic material such as Courlene (polythene) it will not rot or absorb moisture, and it is light and quite cheap. For good measure the settee base is slatted to let air pass through, which also helps to prevent mildew.

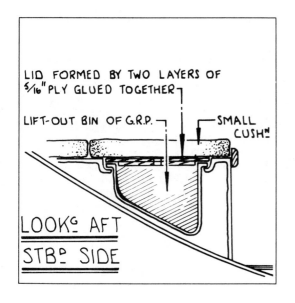

LID FORMED BY TWO LAYERS OF
5/16" PLY GLUED TOGETHER

LIFT-OUT BIN OF G.R.P.   SMALL
                               CUSHⁿ

LOOKᴳ AFT
STBᴰ SIDE

Locker liner   Although the lift-out bin shown
was originally designed for a 30-footer, it
immediately suggests itself for even smaller
boats without deep bilges, where the contents
of lockers under settees tend to get wet from
slopping bilgewater or condensation and
'weeps' inside the hull. The container is ideal
for keeping bread, cakes, meat etc; it can also be
used as a short-term icebox. The bin is made of
GRP and drops into place beneath a small
cushion.

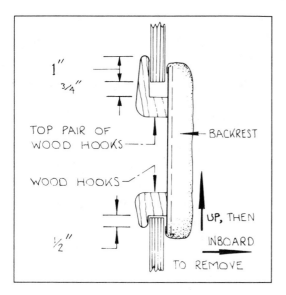

1"
3/4"

TOP PAIR OF
WOOD HOOKS   — BACKREST

WOOD HOOKS

1/2"   UP, THEN

                               INBOARD

                    TO REMOVE

Locker traps   Where there is a plywood back
to a settee berth it is usual to make the space
behind into a locker or series of lockers. Access
will normally be through the front, possibly
with the settee backrest forming the locker door.
The design shown has no hinges or other metal
parts and has the virtue of great simplicity. The
backrest itself is a plywood panel upholstered
on the inboard side. On the outboard
side there are pairs of blunt wooden hooks
which engage on the ply panelling.
The size of the hooks is critical since the
backrest must first be slipped in upwards,
engaging the upper pairs of hooks, and then
dropped vertically so that the bottom pair
latch on. To remove the locker door the process
is reversed.

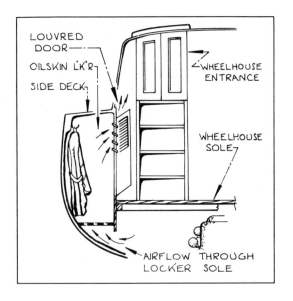

Space stealer   The shape of a human being is wider at the top than at the feet, so any passageway needs to be wide at shoulder and hip level but can taper to quite a narrow width at the bottom. Taking advantage of this, an extra locker can sometimes be worked in by the hanging locker so often placed opposite the toilet, forward of the saloon. It will not be very wide athwartships but it can be quite deep, possibly 18–20 in. The top might be left open for dropping in deck shoes or safety harness and the bottom used for lifejackets or possibly sea-boots, though it is a little awkward for the latter. The top section may have a hinged or lift-off lid, and could serve as the first step up to a forehatch.

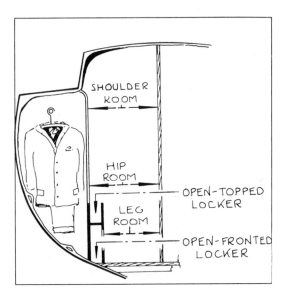

Oily locker   The ideal place for stowing wet oilskins is near the companionway to the deck. This avoids getting drips from oilies all over the cabin, and also it is convenient for anyone rushing on deck in an emergency.

Under the side deck is an area which is not easy to use for many purposes, so it suits the job of oily locker. The bottom can be lower than the sole, making a good place for keeping sea boots. The sole might be of ply with a pattern of 1 in diameter drain and ventilation holes. To allow air circulation there must be slats over a good depth of the locker doors; a door with louvred slats is better than an open locker in helping to muffle noise where warm engineroom air is allowed to circulate through the locker.

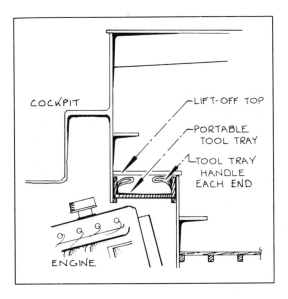

COCKPIT

LIFT-OFF TOP

PORTABLE
TOOL TRAY

TOOL TRAY
HANDLE
EACH END

ENGINE

Tool tray   The best stowage for tools, other than a rack of clips for each tool, is a wide tray. If it is not too deep each item can be seen, and there is less chance of damage to edged tools if they are not underneath a pile. The tray here is over the engine and the warmth helps to keep away rust. The whole tray can be lifted out with the internal strap handles and carried to the job. Combined with its lift-off top this type of tray helps to form a double sound barrier, and yet access to the top of the engine is quick and easy. Over many engines there will be enough width or depth for two or three of these trays.

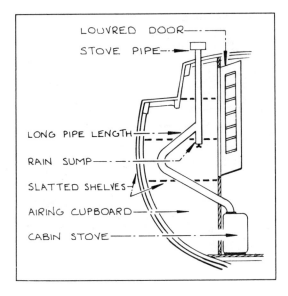

LOUVRED DOOR

STOVE PIPE

LONG PIPE LENGTH

RAIN SUMP

SLATTED SHELVES

AIRING CUPBOARD

CABIN STOVE

Cabin heating   If the pipe from a cabin stove is made as long as possible it will give out the maximum amount of heat inside the boat. However it should not be angled at more than 45° from the vertical or it will not draw easily.

The chimney is shown with a vertical section ending in a sump to catch rainwater, and spray; it has a drain plug at the bottom. The locker enclosing the chimney makes a marvelous airing cupboard, though some care must be taken to avoid singeing clothes. A lot of shelves are needed, and they should be made of slats about 1 in wide with $\frac{1}{2}$ in gaps. The door should have slots to let the rising hot air out, and there must be an air inlet near the bottom. The chimney must be fitted securely otherwise there will soon be rain and smoke leaks.

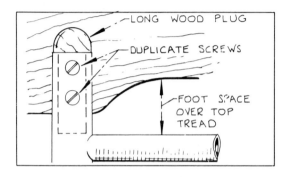

LONG WOOD PLUG

DUPLICATE SCREWS

FOOT SPACE OVER TOP TREAD

Ladder top   Where a ladder is used to give access to a hatch it is important to secure the top very thoroughly since failure here results in sudden, unpleasant accidents. If the ladder cannot be bolted, duplicate screws through the top should be used each side. The tube ends are plugged with well-fitting hardwood plugs which extend well past the screws. When the wood dries it may loosen unless properly secured to an ample length.

The top tread or bar should be as high as possible, leaving space between the coaming and the top of the tread for a foot. In this sketch the coaming has been cut away, giving a minimum foot space of about 5 in.

Most ladders are made of 1 in diameter tube though a short one might be of $\frac{3}{4}$ in tube with $\frac{1}{8}$ in walls.

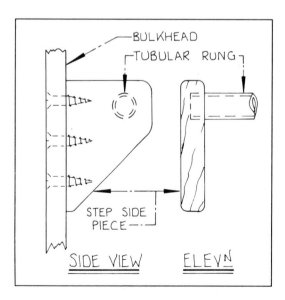

BULKHEAD

TUBULAR RUNG

STEP SIDE PIECE

SIDE VIEW   ELEV^N

Forepeak steps   If a step tread is made of wood it tends to get chafed and worn, particularly when there is sand on the underside of the crew's shoes. Steps made of brass, steel or aluminium tube stand up better to the grinding; 1 or $\frac{3}{4}$ in tube is suitable. This very simple type of individual step is made from tube supported by inch-thick hardwood, secured with three or more screws each side through a bulkhead which should be of $\frac{5}{8}$ in ply or heavier. If the bulkhead is lighter it will need local stiffening.

This type of step can be put in just where convenient, and the whole series need not be in a vertical line if the accommodation makes this difficult. After the steps have been made a heavy man should bounce up and down on each one in turn to make sure that it is going to stand rough sea conditions.

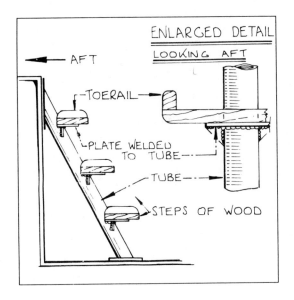

ENLARGED DETAIL

LOOKING AFT

AFT

TOERAIL

PLATE WELDED TO TUBE

TUBE

STEPS OF WOOD

Companion steps   A companionway ladder made from a single tube is not just an unusually light fitting. It also gives easy access to the space aft of the ladder where oilskins, tools or even sails may be stowed. The tube must have plates welded on for each tread, and the plates need triangulating to prevent them tilting or working loose. There have to be toerails at each end of every tread otherwise feet will too easily slide off, especially in rough conditions. Another important detail is the large end plate, at top and bottom ; both of these should be secured with a minimum of three fastenings each.

A comparable ladder, but made out of two tubes, is also shown. The tubes have plates welded on to take the treads, which should ideally be of unvarnished teak. The top tread is stoutly hinged to the bridge deck so that the ladder can be lifted up for access. Oilskins can be grabbed by reaching round either side of a narrow ladder on most boats ; the tool chest shown can be opened without moving the ladder because the lid is narrower than the treads. To repaint or otherwise carry out extensive work behind the ladder the whole contrivance is removed conveniently by withdrawing the hinge pins, which should be a self-holding type such as drop-nose pins or clevis pins.

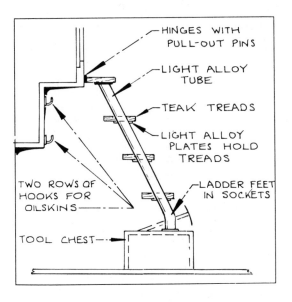

HINGES WITH PULL-OUT PINS

LIGHT ALLOY TUBE

TEAK TREADS

LIGHT ALLOY PLATES HOLD TREADS

TWO ROWS OF HOOKS FOR OILSKINS

LADDER FEET IN SOCKETS

TOOL CHEST

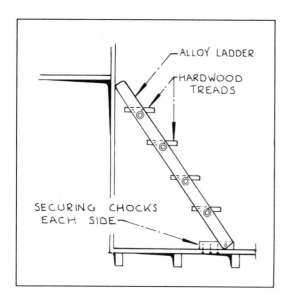

ALLOY LADDER

HARDWOOD TREADS

SECURING CHOCKS EACH SIDE

Light ladder   To make a light, simple companionway ladder buy an ordinary aluminium ladder and cut it to the right length. Fit teak treads over each rung, taking care that they are at an angle so as to be horizontal when the ladder is installed. To secure the wooden treads two stainless or galvanized screws each end are adequate. The bottom end is held by a chock at each upright. To gain access to the area behind the ladder it might be unpinned from the base and lifted away entirely, or pivoted forward and laid on the cabin sole. In order to have clearance for tilting forward the lower ends of the ladder will have to be mounted somewhat off the sole.

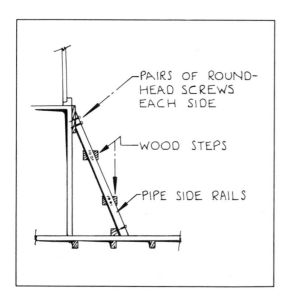

PAIRS OF ROUND-HEAD SCREWS EACH SIDE

WOOD STEPS

PIPE SIDE RAILS

Unusual companionway   Not everyone has welding and brazing facilities, and not everyone can make good joins in wood or metal. This ladder was designed to look attractive and to be extremely simple to fabricate. The sides are made of tube, possibly 2 in brass, and kept well polished or chromed. The treads are of teak and secured by pairs of heavy screws each side. At top and bottom the ladder is secured by the same heavy gauge round-head screws. The steps should have plenty of depth to take two or possibly three screws; the thickness might be $2\frac{1}{2}$ in for two screws and 3 in for three. The screws themselves should be thick, say $\frac{1}{4}$ in diameter, and extend at least 2 in into the wood.

    To save weight aluminium tube could be used, in which case the screws should be of stainless steel. Even galvanized steel piping might be used, but it is harder to drill and should be painted as it does not look smart if left bare.

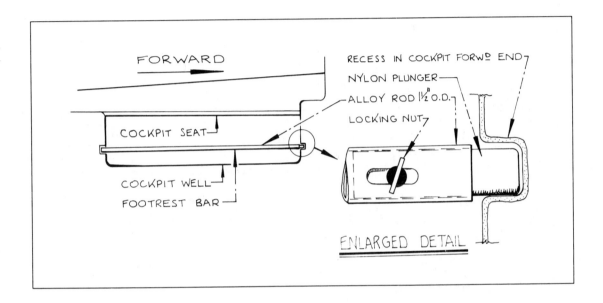

FORWARD

RECESS IN COCKPIT FORWᴰ END
NYLON PLUNGER
ALLOY ROD 1½" O.D.
LOCKING NUT

COCKPIT SEAT

COCKPIT WELL
FOOTREST BAR

ENLARGED DETAIL

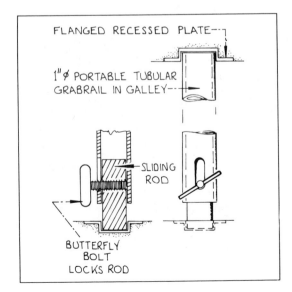

FLANGED RECESSED PLATE

1" ⌀ PORTABLE TUBULAR
GRABRAIL IN GALLEY

SLIDING
ROD

BUTTERFLY
BOLT
LOCKS ROD

A portable grabrail Useful in the galley, toilet area or elsewhere, the rail can be removed to give extra space and a sense of roominess in harbour. It can be mounted vertically or horizontally, and in the cockpit provides a footrest when the boat is heeled and the cockpit is too wide to allow the crew to brace themselves against the leeward seats.

The rail consists of a 1 in diameter bright metal tube with a slot at one end through which there is a butterfly bolt. The bolt is threaded through a short sliding rod which locks the rail into recessed end plates. Where the rail is mounted between GRP mouldings it may have a short nylon inner rod which engages a moulded recess without damaging it.

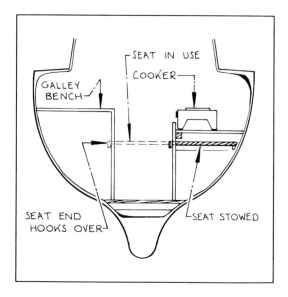

Cook's seat   Make this seat from a piece of hardwood about 10 in wide and 1½ in thick. Cut a slot in the locker fronts on each side of the centre passageway, the slots being exactly the same height and precisely opposite each other. The seat slides outboard to be stowed away and a downwards lip on the end of the seat prevents it sliding too far outboard; this same lip engages in the panel opposite when it is in position. The seat should be fitted on drawer slides to guide it into the stowed position. Anyone sitting on the seat can face forward or aft, or sit astride. The same type of seat can be used for the navigator or can be located in the companionway.

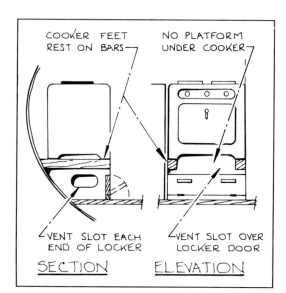

Cleaner galley   The space under a stove is hard to keep clean because it is so small. It normally extends the full width and depth of the stove, but is too shallow to get a hand all the way in. The usual arrangement is with the stove standing on a shelf, so that its top is level with the other galley working surfaces. However there is no reason why the feet should be on a complete shelf: they could stand on wood strips with a clear gap between. The locker under the stove would then have a slightly greater depth, cooling round the stove would be better, and cleaning under it would merely consist of cleaning out the locker, which is simple. It has to be admitted that the locker cannot be used for perishables, but it will be suitable for pots and pans, and the wide gap at the top makes it easier to remove and replace them without opening the locker front. It may also make it easier to run the gas piping, and improve access to the shut-off valve.

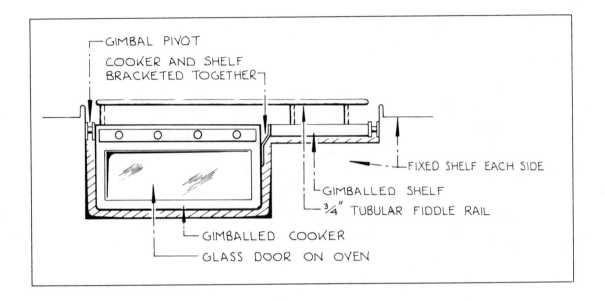

GIMBAL PIVOT

COOKER AND SHELF
BRACKETED TOGETHER

FIXED SHELF EACH SIDE

GIMBALLED SHELF

¾" TUBULAR FIDDLE RAIL

GIMBALLED COOKER

GLASS DOOR ON OVEN

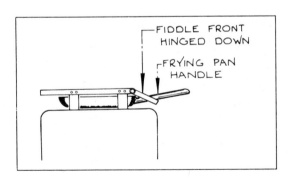

FIDDLE FRONT
HINGED DOWN

FRYING PAN
HANDLE

Gimballed work surface When a cooker is secured to a shelf and the whole unit gimballed, pots can be taken off the stove and set down on an adjacent horizontal surface regardless of the angle of heel. This is particularly convenient when pouring or ladling liquids. The tubular fiddle shown is stronger and neater than the flat bar fiddles which are almost universally fitted on cookers.

The smaller sketch shows how frying pans can be held safely yet completely flat on a stove.

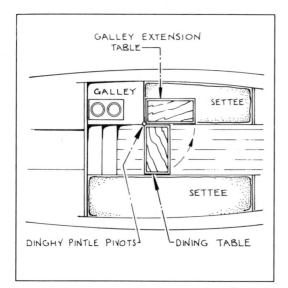

Swing table   While a meal is being prepared there is always a shortage of 'setting down' space in the galley, even on quite large yachts. Once the meal is ready, it is dining table area which is needed. The simple arrangement here has been designed so that the galley extension can be swung readily athwartships to become a dining table. In the layout shown it will seat three, one to port and one each side to starboard. The plates and mugs can be filled when the table is adjacent to the galley, before swinging the whole meal into the 'eating position'.

   Naturally a table like this needs sturdy pivots. Standard dinghy gudgeons and pintles serve very well. There must be an upper and lower set, but then this applies to any form of hingeing. A single hinge is no good, as every youngster discovers when he makes his first rabbit hutch.

Temporary tables   In the Folkboat *Fair Breeze* there are two clever tables. They are identical, about 15 in fore and aft, and approximately the same width as the settee berths in the saloon. They look much like trays, as they have fiddles all round.

   When the owner wants to do a lot of cooking he adds both tables to the forward end of the galley, in positions (1) and (2), to extend the working area. When the meal is cooked he shifts the tables to (3) and (4) so that people can sit each side of each table. If there are only three people aboard, he can leave one table at (1) and put the other at (4), making three dining places, one doubling as an extension to the galley. As a bonus, each table is small enough to stow easily, simple to use and easy to make.

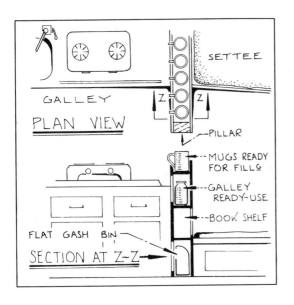

SETTEE

GALLEY

PLAN VIEW

Z   Z

--PILLAR

--MUGS READY
FOR FILLS

--GALLEY
READY-USE

--BOOK SHELF

FLAT GASH BIN

SECTION AT Z~Z---

Slim store   Partial bulkheads between the galley or chart area and the saloon settee are often seen. Sometimes there is a pillar on the end of this bulkhead to support the cabin top. If a light bulkhead is fixed to the forward face of this pillar and another to the aft face, the space between can be used as a particularly well-placed stowage area. The deep trough along the top can hold mugs ready for filling ; once full, one can be set there for the person on the end of the settee. The next shelf down is a good place for jars and bottles, being taller than the stowage under the galley working sur-face. Below that there may be a book shelf, or the space may be used to stow bedding or even to make the settee berth a few inches longer. The bottom space holds a slim gash bucket.

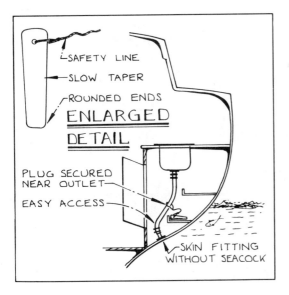

-SAFETY LINE

-SLOW TAPER

-ROUNDED ENDS

ENLARGED
DETAIL

PLUG SECURED
NEAR OUTLET---

EASY ACCESS---

-SKIN FITTING
WITHOUT SEACOCK

Bungs for cruisers   A great many small cruisers are now being built with no seacocks on hull outlets and inlets. This would not be so bad if the openings were near the waterline where they could be plugged, perhaps with difficulty, from the outside by hanging down from the deck, but many of them are right down near the garboards.

The proper cure for this situation is to fit a seacock. However, if this is too expensive, at least anticipate trouble and make up a softwood plug for each opening. The plug should have a slight taper and the ends rounded at the bottom for easy entry and at the top to avoid splitting when being hammered home. Each plug should be hung by a lanyard from its own pipe. Offshore racing rules often require such plugs for all hull openings even on boats where seacocks are fitted.

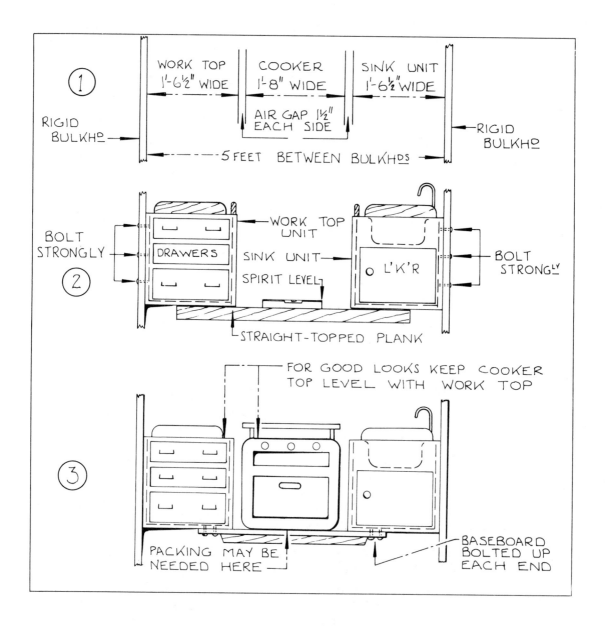

① WORK TOP 1'-6½" WIDE   COOKER 1'-8" WIDE   SINK UNIT 1'-6½" WIDE
RIGID BULKHᴰ   AIR GAP 1½" EACH SIDE   RIGID BULKHᴰ
5 FEET BETWEEN BULKHᴰˢ

② BOLT STRONGLY   WORK TOP UNIT   SINK UNIT   SPIRIT LEVEL   DRAWERS   L'K'R   BOLT STRONGLʸ
STRAIGHT-TOPPED PLANK

③ FOR GOOD LOOKS KEEP COOKER TOP LEVEL WITH WORK TOP
PACKING MAY BE NEEDED HERE   BASEBOARD BOLTED UP EACH END

Fitting furniture   For both amateur and
professional boatbuilding it is often more
economical to assemble furniture away from the
boat and fit each unit in place as a completed
unit. An example of a galley made this way is
shown. It consists of three parts, not including
the stove ; there is a worktop unit with three
drawers, a sink unit complete with pumps, sink
and locker, and the baseboard for the cooker.

The first sketch shows how the available space
is carefully measured up. An air gap each side of
the cooker takes into account any slight dis-
crepancies in construction and measurement.
If a series of boats is being built it is probable
that the gap between the bulkheads will vary
slightly, but this error should not be more than
1 in and the air gaps beside the cooker cater
for this. The air gap has an insulating effect,
and additional insulation can be added later if
desired.

The made-up units are then bolted on (2).
The work unit has been secured to the bulkhead
and the sink unit carefully lined up with it using
a straightedge and spirit level. Generally, a
minimum of six bolts will be used for each unit
the back of which will be shaped to follow the
contour of the boat's topsides. Tight fitting at
the back of which will be shaped to follow the
whole complex is raised well clear of the sole.

The third drawing shows the baseboard bolted
up against the left and right hand units. The
baseboard might consist of a pair of $4 \times \frac{5}{8}$ in
mahogany planks each stiffened by a $3 \times \frac{5}{8}$ in
vertical piece, to make a T-section. The cooker is
bolted to the baseboards which have previously
been bolted to the left and right hand units
using a minimum of three bolts each end. To
improve the appearance the baseboard should
be set in so that it can be seen only by kneeling
down until the eye is level with it.

Naturally, each unit must be small enough to
pass through the companionway. In practice,
some small packing pieces may be needed to
line up the units and these should be made of
matching hardwood.

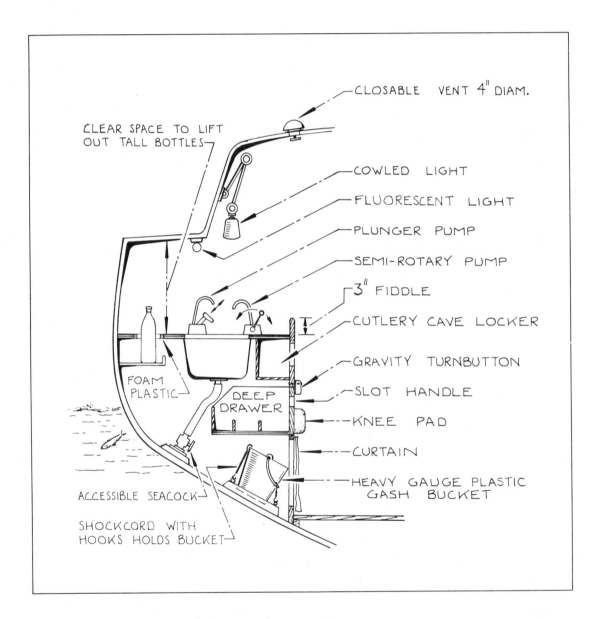

Galley design   When designing a new
galley or replanning an existing one, these
ideas may be useful.

Heat, steam and smells come from the stove
and a vent is needed over the galley to clear the
air; the mushroom vent has much to recommend
it since it can be closed in rough weather.
However, any vent of less than 4 in tends to be
ineffective and two may be needed.

It is usual to have a cowled light over the
chart table so that the navigator does not disturb others in the cabin, or the cockpit
crew's night vision. The same applies to the
galley light, and if it can be moved about it
becomes more useful. A shaded fluorescent
light has some of the advantages of a movable
light as its illumination comes from a long length
of tube. It is also economical in its use of
electricity.

When salt and fresh water pumps are installed
it is better to have the salt supply nearer the
cook so that the natural tendency is to use it
and so save valuable fresh water. Of the two
types shown the plunger pump is far less reliable
than the rotary type with the stubby lever, which
admittedly costs more. The plunger type is
liable to get a bent rod if the cook is clutching
the handle when the boat rolls and his weight is
held by the too-delicate pump. The sink
seacock has its handle inboard to be as accessible as possible, and should be turned off
whenever the yacht is left unattended.

Sometimes there is a small and normally useless space under the galley worktops such as that
between the sink and the front panel. This can be
made into an open-fronted cave locker for cutlery
or cooking implements.

There are various tricks for holding drawers
and lockers shut. One of the best is the gravity
turnbutton (detailed elsewhere) which is
nothing more than a strong, loosely-pivoted
chock which drops down whenever it is
released.

The deep drawer shown is particularly
useful for stowing anything from jam jars to

sauce bottles. The sides are cut away
at the top outboard edge to clear the sink
plumbing, and there are deep fiddles inside to
stop the contents rattling and to prevent the
taller bottles from sliding outboard and fouling
the sink. On the front of the drawer is a knee
pad; underneath is an open-fronted space for
the garbage bucket, held in place with
shockcord.

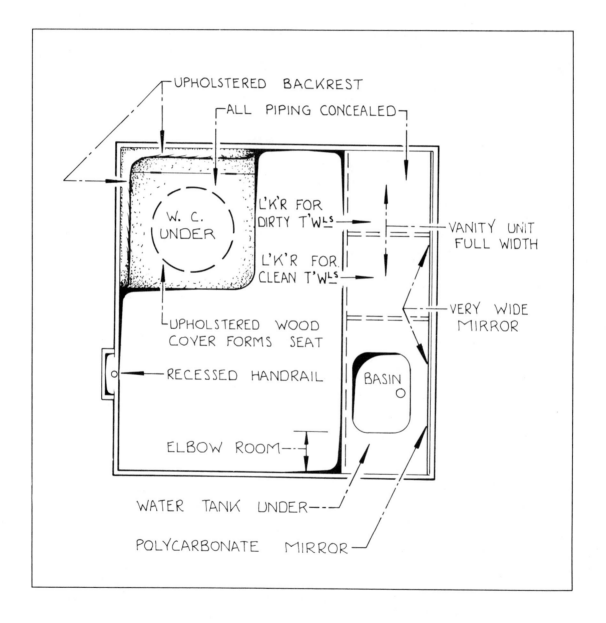

UPHOLSTERED BACKREST

ALL PIPING CONCEALED

W. C.
UNDER

L'K'R FOR
DIRTY T'W^{LS}

L'K'R FOR.
CLEAN T'W^{LS}

VANITY UNIT
FULL WIDTH

VERY WIDE
MIRROR

UPHOLSTERED WOOD
COVER FORMS SEAT

RECESSED HANDRAIL

BASIN

ELBOW ROOM

WATER TANK UNDER

POLYCARBONATE   MIRROR

Lessons from aircraft   There are vast
differences between ergonomic considerations
of layout design in boats and in aeroplanes.
Nevertheless, the styling and ingenuity displayed
by aircraft designers can provide useful inspira-
tion. Shown here is a plan view of a typical
aircraft toilet compartment. Whereas yacht
toilet seats are fragile and often break, on aircraft
these appear to be of plywood covered with a
$\frac{1}{4}$ in thickness of soft plastic foam and a
washable leathercloth material. The casing
around the toilet conceals the piping and valves,
just as the vanity unit hides the plumbing to the
basin.

Two lockers or drawers in the vanity unit are
for clean and dirty linen and the wall space above
is faced with a large mirror. This mirror may be
of polycarbonate (Makrolon), which is
unbreakable and light in weight. It can be cut
to shape and drilled with ordinary metal working
tools. The basin is kept away from the bulkhead
at the base of the plan to give sufficient
elbowroom, otherwise washing is most awkward.
By recessing the handrail the feeling of space is
enhanced and the chances of bruising are
reduced.

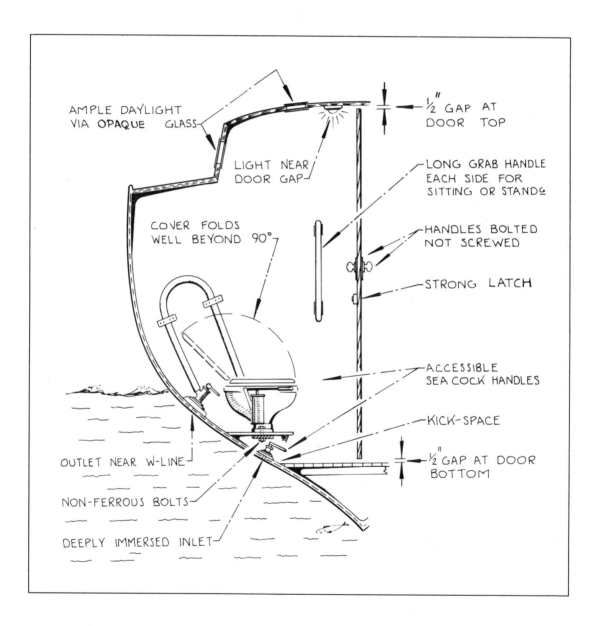

AMPLE DAYLIGHT
VIA **OPAQUE** GLASS

LIGHT NEAR
DOOR GAP

COVER FOLDS
WELL BEYOND 90°

OUTLET NEAR W-LINE

NON-FERROUS BOLTS

DEEPLY IMMERSED INLET

$\frac{1}{2}''$ GAP AT
DOOR TOP

LONG GRAB HANDLE
EACH SIDE FOR
SITTING OR STANDG

HANDLES BOLTED
NOT SCREWED

STRONG LATCH

ACCESSIBLE
SEA COCK HANDLES

KICK-SPACE

$\frac{1}{2}''$ GAP AT DOOR
BOTTOM

Toilet area   A single porthole in the heads compartment is seldom enough for ventilation or light. A deadlight fitted through the coach-roof or side deck can make all the difference. If a good gap is left between the top and bottom of the door and the frame or bulkhead it will aid air circulation, and if the light is left on accidentally it will be noticed. Another reason for the gaps is that since boats work a certain amount, particularly when driven hard, they prevent the door from jamming or squeaking.

The door furniture should be very strong to prevent it being distorted or broken in bad weather, and through-bolted handrails on each side of the compartment are essential. The toilet lid should fold back well beyond 90° so that even when heeled steeply it will not slam shut.

Seacocks for the system should be located so that effluent will not be sucked back in via the clean water inlets for the handbasin, galley sink, or toilet. It is a distressing fact that inlets for galley and handbasin salt water pumps are sometimes fitted on the same side of the hull and aft of toilet discharge openings. No more comment is needed! If the large w.c. outlet pipe is fitted through the hull fairly near the waterline it can be plugged from outside in the event of damage. However the clean water inlet should be well immersed and down near the keel to prevent it sucking air.

Tenders and Equipment

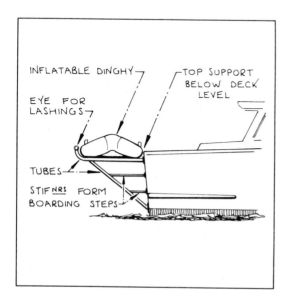

INFLATABLE DINGHY

EYE FOR LASHINGS

TOP SUPPORT BELOW DECK LEVEL

TUBES

STIF<u>NRS</u> FORM BOARDING STEPS

Carrying an inflatable   If the dinghy is carried aft it does not obstruct the helmsman's vision; also it is positioned conveniently for hauling aboard and launching. These two sketches show power yachts, but the basic ideas could be used on sailing yachts.

The top sketch shows a permanent platform made of tubing bolted to the transom. It must be strong enough to support the dinghy when full of rainwater, and there must be tubes athwart-ships or diagonally from the outreaching arms to the transom, to prevent any sideways movement.

It has to be admitted that the fixed structure shown is obtrusive and could be a menace in a canal or dock. The alternative shown has a great deal to commend it, not least its better appearance. It is probably easier to fit, and could have metal tubular retractable arms instead of the wooden ones shown.

Naturally the dinghy must be well lashed down on each side and at both ends, otherwise it will blow away. To prevent spray and rain accumulating it may be secured upside down, but this will not be so convenient for launching in a hurry.

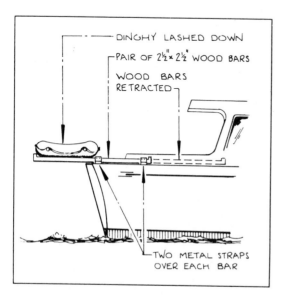

DINGHY LASHED DOWN

PAIR OF 2½" x 2½" WOOD BARS

WOOD BARS RETRACTED

TWO METAL STRAPS OVER EACH BAR

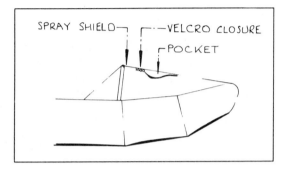

Dinghy stowage   One of the troubles with inflatables is that they lack lockers or other places to stow loose gear. Where they are used as tenders and travel some distance between the parent yacht and the shore it is a good idea to carry a torch, a whistle and small compass in case of fog, and perhaps a couple of flares. Also there are often small packages or articles of clothing that would suffer from a wetting if they were set down in the bottom.

One way of devising stowage space is to make a pocket inside the spray shield; it can be sewn to the shield and closed with a Velcro strip. The pocket is not obvious so pilfering is unlikely, and as it is high up it is well away from water in the bottom and careless feet.

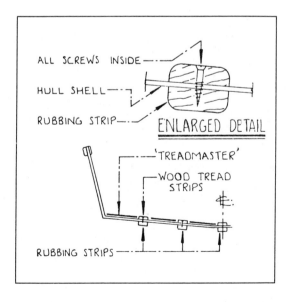

For fibreglass or ply   The aim of this treatment of the bottom of a dinghy or tender is to stiffen the shell, provide some protection against abrasion, and make it easier to stand up inside. The rubbing strips are fastened from the inside by screws, so that when the wood wears away the heads of the screws are not taken off. Although the screws may eventually be damaged at their points this will not make them impossible to remove. The tread strips inside the boat stop the feet slipping sideways and also stiffen the bottom. Between the strips a heavy-pattern non-skid deck covering material (such as Treadmaster, used by the RNLI) wears well, prevents slipping and looks neat.

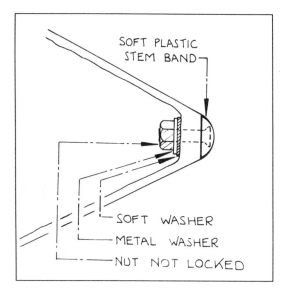

SOFT PLASTIC
STEM BAND

SOFT WASHER
METAL WASHER
NUT NOT LOCKED

Replaceable nose   A fibreglass hull is easily chipped where it is resin rich, in places such as the forward side of the stem. A soft plastic stem band is light, cheap, easy to fit, and to a certain extent will cushion any blow. It must be secured by close-spaced bolts which must not have locked nuts because renewal is likely to be required every three to five years—sometimes more often.

If the stem band is not in one piece, the join should be below the waterline, for neatness. The bolts need soft washers which will bed tightly onto the uneven inner face of the fibreglass shell. They should be of the same material as the other immersed metal fittings, to avoid electrolytic action.

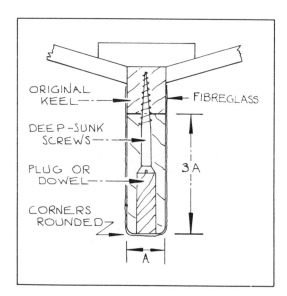

ORIGINAL
KEEL
FIBREGLASS

DEEP-SUNK
SCREWS

PLUG OR
DOWEL

3 A

CORNERS
ROUNDED

A

Deepening a skeg   If a dinghy needs a deeper skeg or keel, one way of doing the job is shown in this sketch. The addition is made the same width as the existing keel. Holes are drilled about every 6 in in the new piece, so that the screw heads can be sunk well in. If this is not done it will be necessary to obtain very long screws, and this can be difficult and pricey.

The screws have to be driven carefully so that they go well into the original keel without penetrating right through. The screw holes are plugged with wood or a filler; the outer sheathing of fibreglass stiffens and waterproofs the whole addition. The depth of the added piece should not be much more than three times its width, to avoid coggling.

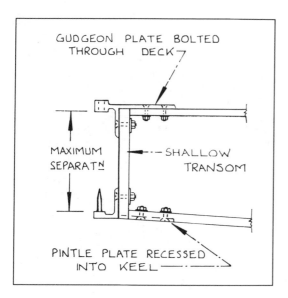

GUDGEON PLATE BOLTED
THROUGH DECK

MAXIMUM
SEPARAT.ᴺ

SHALLOW
TRANSOM

PINTLE PLATE RECESSED
INTO KEEL

Retaining the rudder   Some modern dinghies and small cats have very shallow transoms, which means that the gap between the upper and lower rudder fittings is small and so the loadings may be extremely high.

If the fittings are bolted through the transom they may have to be almost touching, to allow for the flange widths, since the external flanges on the fittings must not project below the bottom or above the top of the transom. The sketch shows a set of specially made fittings which will provide a much more secure attachment, since the fittings are separated as much as possible and also fastened to the keel and after deck.

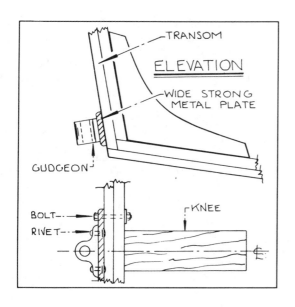

TRANSOM

ELEVATION

WIDE STRONG
METAL PLATE

GUDGEON

BOLT
RIVET
KNEE

Rugged gudgeon   When a rudder hits the seabed there is a tremendous strain on the lower rudder fitting. Dinghies with the gudgeon near the bottom of the transom are particularly vulnerable. It is essential to bolt the lower fittings in place, but this can sometimes be difficult. One reason why bolts cannot be used is the presence of a stern knee which is wider than the gap between fastening holes in the transom fitting. The overcome this the gudgeon is secured to a metal plate which is bolted to the transom. The idea has a wide variety of applications; for instance, some deck fittings have fastenings which are too close together, particularly for use on light fibreglass panels. Where possible the metal plate should be of the same material as the fitting.

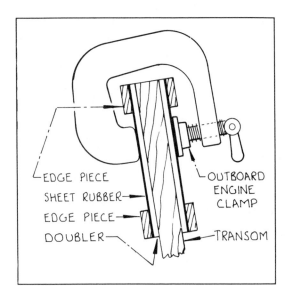

Transom pad　　Outboard motor clamps tend to bite into any transom, leaving at least an ugly mark and sometimes appreciable damage. To prevent this the transom is fitted with a pair of doublers which absorb any crushing effect when the clamps are tightened. On top of the doublers are sheets of rubber such as the tough type used for stair treads. The edge pieces secure the rubber, and the top one also prevents the motor working itself up over the edge if the clamps are slightly loose.

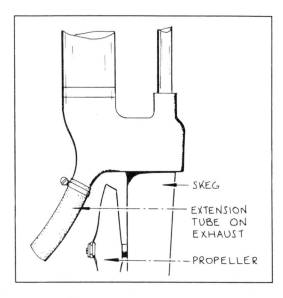

Outboard exhaust fumes　　Under cruising conditions exhaust often tends to waft up inside the engine well and into the cockpit, and even the cabin. The remedy shown is for a Seagull and consists of nothing more than a short length of curved tube fitted to the exhaust outlet and held by a hose clamp. This carries the fumes down into the propeller wash.

　　Some engines on which the exhaust outlet is underwater have a cooling water outlet above the waterline which also emits fumes. This can be dealt with by adding a shaped copper plate on which a $\frac{3}{4}$ in o.d. stub of tube has been brazed, to take a length of clear plastic tubing that extends below the water level. The plate can be held on with hose clamps. To reduce back pressure when starting, the tube can be bent up clear of the water. Noise is reduced also, and the cooling water flow is visible through the clear plastic.

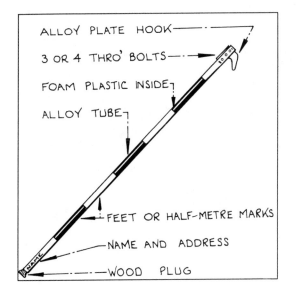

ALLOY PLATE HOOK

3 OR 4 THRO' BOLTS

FOAM PLASTIC INSIDE

ALLOY TUBE

FEET OR HALF-METRE MARKS

NAME AND ADDRESS

WOOD PLUG

Aluminium boathook   A length of 1 in (25 mm) aluminium tube makes a good boathook about 9 ft (3 m) long. If the length needed is only 6 ft (2 m) or so, a piece of $\frac{3}{4}$ in (18 mm) tube is adequate. The top is slit and a piece of $\frac{1}{4}$ in (6 mm) aluminium plate cut to the shape of a hook is slipped in, and held by three bolts. Coat the whole end with epoxy paint to inhibit corrosion, and on no account use bolts containing copper, as all brasses and bronzes do.

To make the boathook float when it drops overboard it should have strips of buoyant plastic foam slid inside. The ends can then be sealed, but in practice the foam will support the pole without bothering to seal the ends. The marks on the pole are for sounding and are in whatever system of units matches the chart soundings (feet or metres). The owner's name and address can be painted on.

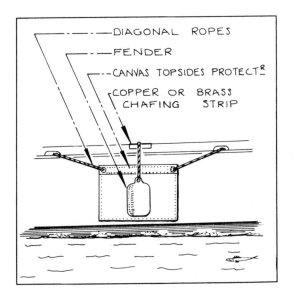

DIAGONAL ROPES

FENDER

CANVAS TOPSIDES PROTECT^R

COPPER OR BRASS CHAFING STRIP

Aprons for the topsides   When a boat lies alongside for a long period the fenders may score the topsides. If there is any grit between the hull and the fender scratching can become quite serious over one or two seasons. Fastidious owners can fit canvas aprons inside each fender to preserve the pristine appearance of the hull. These aprons need two well-spread diagonal hanging ropes to prevent the canvas shifting fore and aft. The fender itself will move about whenever the yacht shifts and for this reason its ropes should not be left hanging over an unprotected toerail. There should either be a fairlead or a chafing strip to prevent the rope wearing away the rail or its protective finish.

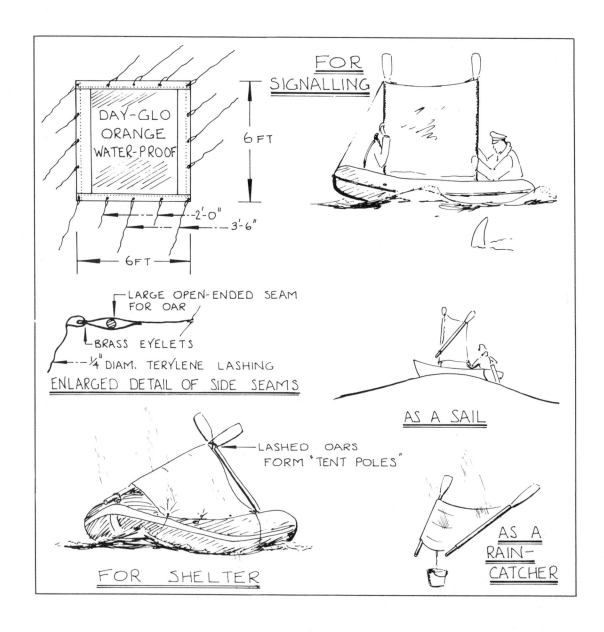

DAY-GLO
ORANGE
WATER-PROOF

6 FT

2'-0"

3'-6"

6 FT

FOR
SIGNALLING

LARGE OPEN-ENDED SEAM
FOR OAR

BRASS EYELETS

¼" DIAM. TERYLENE LASHING

ENLARGED DETAIL OF SIDE SEAMS

AS A SAIL

LASHED OARS
FORM "TENT POLES"

FOR SHELTER

AS A
RAIN-
CATCHER

Safety sheet   So much safety equipment is
expensive, and in the course of time becomes
useless. Flares, fire extinguishers, inflatable
liferafts and lifejackets all have quite a limited
life. A safety sheet, on the other hand, is inexpensive to make and should last almost
indefinitely. It can be kept stowed in the
yacht's cockpit but will probably be better left
permanently in the dinghy. In practice there are
more true accidents and uncomfortable situations
concerning dinghies than yachts. People get
lost in fog rowing ashore, they get swept off
downtide when trying to row out to their boats,
oars go overboard, and so on. In any of these
situations a safety sheet will be a great help in
ensuring survival and bringing help more quickly.
    The actual size and construction can be varied
to suit different situations. The sheet might
be designed to fit over the forward part of a
particular dinghy and lashed permanently in place
to give extra 'deck' forward. Alternatively it
could be made in the form of a simple sail with
extra eyelets all round. The lanyards shown are
perhaps rather more numerous than seems essential, but for lashing in severe weather it is
necessary to have close-spaced ties which
are amply strong.
    For long life the fabric, stitching and lashings
should be of a synthetic such as Terylene
(Dacron) painted with Day-Glo fluorescent
orange.

Fitting Out

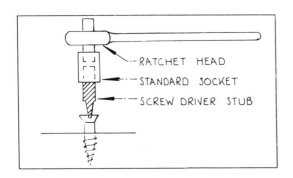

RATCHET HEAD
STANDARD SOCKET
SCREW DRIVER STUB

Socket screwdriver A handy addition to any set of sockets is a screwdriver bit which can be used with the ratchet handle and one of the standard sockets. One way to make up the screwdriver stub is to grind a blade end on an Allen key. If this cannot be found then it may be worth taking the end off a screwdriver. Ordinary stub screwdrivers, so valuable for working underneath w.c.s and in other confined spaces. are relatively ineffective for seized screws, whereas a ratchet handle on a standard socket gives a very powerful twisting action.

It is worth making a slot in inaccessible bolt heads when installing them so that with this tool the head can be prevented from turning and the nut undone with a spanner.

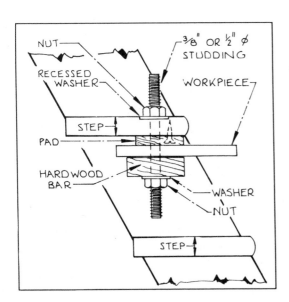

NUT
$\frac{3}{8}''$ OR $\frac{1}{2}'' \phi$ STUDDING
RECESSED WASHER
WORKPIECE
STEP
PAD
HARDWOOD BAR
WASHER
NUT
STEP

A vice Anyone who wants to work on his boat when she is afloat finds life difficult without some sort of vice. This sketch shows an inexpensive light portable vice, made by using the cabin steps as the basis.

One of the steps has two holes drilled in it, and a big washer recessed at the top of each hole. On the underside of the step there is a hardwood pad screwed in position ; for metal-working this pad could be a brass plate. A wide hardwood bar is made, with holes in it to match the holes in the step. The piece of wood or metal which is being worked on is clamped between the underside of the step and the hardwood bar. Threaded rod (studding) is used to haul the bar up tight.

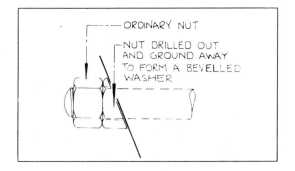

Wedge washer   It is surprisingly difficult to buy wedge washers, and in any case they are normally made up to standard angles such as 30° which do not necessarily suit a particular problem. One way to make up wedge washers is to drill the thread out of a nut, then grind or file it to the correct bevel. This is far better than using an oversize nut which will always be a sloppy fit and does not give the same neat appearance. Remember that if the washer is to be galvanized after drilling and filing, the hole through the middle should be made a good $\frac{1}{16}$ in oversize to allow for the thickness of the galvanizing. The wedge must also be filed to the exact angle or it will damage the very surface it is designed to protect.

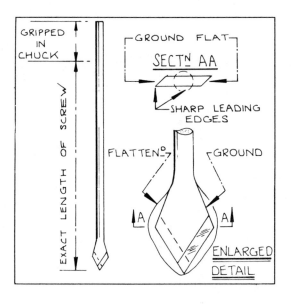

Penny drill   Amateurs and professionals are familiar with the cost of drills. They know those ghastly days when four drills of one size are broken in a morning. For drilling wood for screws, it is easy to make up simple cheap drills from hard wire. Some people use various types of bronze and as a result get a good drill for keeping on a boat since this material does not rust. However this type is only a complete success when used with an electric drill, though it can be used with an ordinary 'hand whirly' wheelbrace.

The end is flattened with a few blows of a hammer, then the edge ground on with an electric grinder or filed to a point. The width of the blade determines the diameter of the hole drilled.

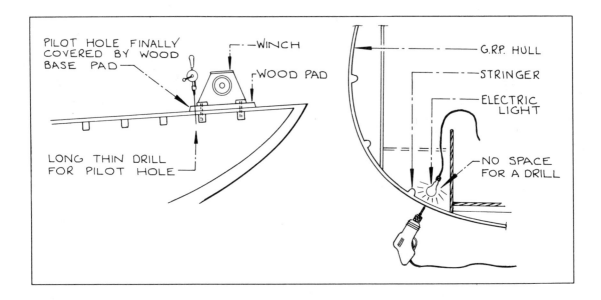

Drilling blind   Working on any craft, all
sorts of problems arise when trying to drill
holes through the deck, hull or furniture.
In the top left sketch a winch is being fitted
on the foredeck and the problem is to ensure
that the holding-down bolts go through the
centres of the deck beams. It is sometimes
impossible to drill upwards; space may be too
cramped to use a drill. In this case the shipwright measures as carefully as he can and
drills down from above. He uses a very thin, long
drill and, as shown, misses the beam completely.
He can now measure from the pilot hole forward
to the beam and then drill the bolt hole correctly.
The pilot hole is sealed up and covered by the
wood pad fitted under the winch.
   In the top right sketch a skin fitting has to
be put in under a berth. There is no room to
drill, and it is important to miss the stringer
and the berth front. Measuring round the

inside of the hull shell is difficult in this case
because of the locker front; otherwise inside and
outside measurements would establish the
correct drilling position. Because this is a
fibreglass hull the shipwright can hold a powerful
electric light exactly where he wants the drill to
come through and it will shine through once the
antifouling is scraped away.

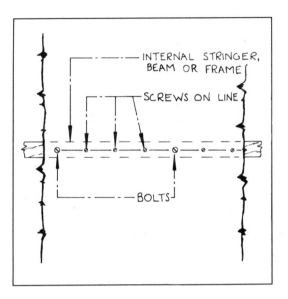

Accurate drilling   Occasionally even professionally built boats from good yards have some bad workmanship. Under the deck, or elsewhere inboard, there are signs that the shipwright has misjudged his drilling when putting in a screw. It may be through the deck into a beam, or through the topsides into a stringer.

To eliminate the risk of this error, a good technique is to use occasional bolts, with screws between. The holes for the bolts are drilled from inside, plumb in the middle of the stringer, or whatever the component is. On the outside, a pencil line is made from the centre of one bolt hole to the next and the screws are driven in exactly through the pencil line. If the stringer has much curve in it, the bolts must not be too far apart, but with practice it is easy to place the screws correctly.

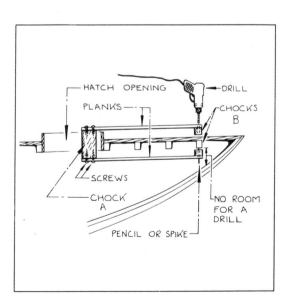

Drilling jig   Two planks are joined by a big chock (A). The two little chocks (B) are fastened to the planks and pre-drilled so that a rod will extend through the upper plank and its chock, then straight on through the lower chock and its plank. The jig can then be taken apart and reassembled with the two arms straddling the deck and chock (A) in the hatchway. While one man holds a pencil or spike through lower chock (B) up to the centre of the scantling the second man drills vertically down through the hole in chock (B), knowing that he will be drilling towards the lower marker.

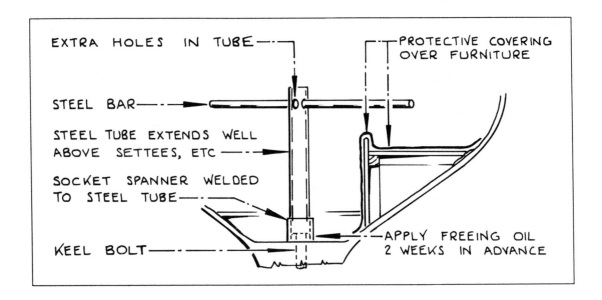

EXTRA HOLES IN TUBE

PROTECTIVE COVERING OVER FURNITURE

STEEL BAR

STEEL TUBE EXTENDS WELL ABOVE SETTEES, ETC

SOCKET SPANNER WELDED TO STEEL TUBE

KEEL BOLT

APPLY FREEING OIL 2 WEEKS IN ADVANCE

Keel bolt spanner   An ordinary spanner (wrench) seldom works when asked to loosen a keel bolt. What is needed is a great big socket spanner, with an absurdly long, strong cross-bar The business end of this spanner is made up of a short socket spanner, just high enough to clear the nut with say an inch extra for safety. The main length is of heavy gauge common steel tube which has holes at the top for the cross-bar. There should be at least two sets of holes, not set at right angles, so that the bar can be shifted from one position to another. Furniture is then less likely to be bumped as the cross-bar is rotated, and the operators can have the best stance.

The nuts should be liberally treated with a freeing oil a week before they are to be loosened and the surrounding furniture should be well covered during the whole operation to prevent damage

This valuable spanner should be kept in the yacht's store, not carried aboard (except on an ocean cruiser) as it is likely to be needed only once every three years. But when it is needed, the matter is likely to be important, and the unavailability of such a tool can be expensive and time-consuming.

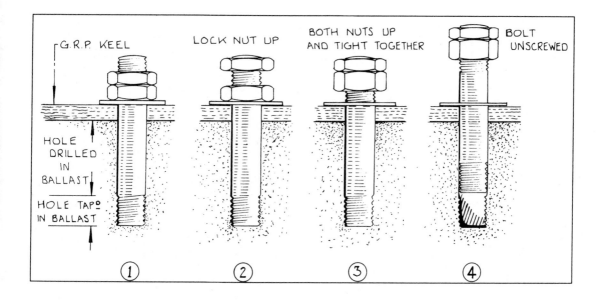

G.R.P. KEEL

LOCK NUT UP

BOTH NUTS UP
AND TIGHT TOGETHER

BOLT
UNSCREWED

HOLE
DRILLED
IN
BALLAST

HOLE TAPᵈ
IN BALLAST

① ② ③ ④

Ballast keelbolts When an external ballast keel is fitted to a fibreglass yacht one of the techniques used for securing it is the headless bolt. This series of sketches shows the method of removing one of these bolts for inspection. The locking nut is first wound up to the top of the bolt. This may only involve turning it a short distance, perhaps two threads. Next the main nut is brought up and hardened against the locking nut. Finally the bolt is wound out by turning the locked main nut and bringing the bolt up in the usual way.

When replacing one of these bolts it is very important to have the shank and thread of the bolt perfectly clean and lightly greased. While the bolt is out the hole should be plugged so that grit, pieces of wood or other foreign material cannot get into the hole.

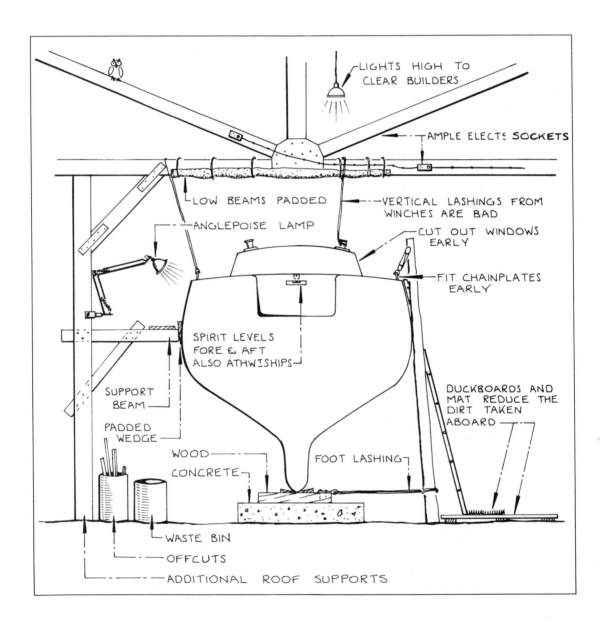

LIGHTS HIGH TO CLEAR BUILDERS

AMPLE ELECT: SOCKETS

LOW BEAMS PADDED

VERTICAL LASHINGS FROM WINCHES ARE BAD

ANGLEPOISE LAMP

CUT OUT WINDOWS EARLY

FIT CHAINPLATES EARLY

SPIRIT LEVELS FORE & AFT ALSO ATHWISHIPS

SUPPORT BEAM

DUCKBOARDS AND MAT REDUCE THE DIRT TAKEN ABOARD

PADDED WEDGE

WOOD

CONCRETE

FOOT LASHING

WASTE BIN

OFFCUTS

ADDITIONAL ROOF SUPPORTS

For building or rebuilding, for altering or just laying up in style   When working on a boat the surroundings need careful thought. Low overhead beams should be padded to minimize head denting ; ideally the padding should be bright orange to warn victims before they actually hit. Suspended lights should be well above head height, and as a result may be too remote for the work. An Anglepoise lamp is often a great help, especially if it has a clamp base which can be screwed onto pillars or beams or parts of the boat.

Wandering leads are best with fairly short cables, so the shed needs ample electric outlets. When drilling it is often a great asset to have one electric drill loaded with a bit and a second with a countersink, which again calls for extra sockets.

A boat should never be set directly on anything unresilient such as concrete or steel rails. Regardless of the hull material the keel should be on wood chocks, though these can often be set on concrete sleepers or steel channels since large lumps of wood may be hard to find. The support needs to be above reproach, for at times there will be half a dozen visitors all standing on one side, creating a serious imbalance. If the chainplates are fitted then tackles from them can be led to overhead beams or to the tops of strong struts. Lashing the boat up by its winches is seldom a good idea because winches are designed for horizontal, not vertical, loads.

Once the boat is well secured she should be carefully lined up athwartships, also fore and aft. To make sure she is right a spirit level is used. A pair of these may be permanently fitted in the cockpit or by the chart table ; it's amazing how many boats are down by the stern, or ride at moorings with a permanent slight list.

When working on a boat it is inevitable that dirt gets taken aboard. But the less muck that goes up the ladder the better, so a set of duckboards and a hairy mat make sense, especially in wet weather. Likewise a 40 gallon drum for rubbish makes the workshop pleasanter and reduces the chances of important components being lost among the shavings. An offcut bin is just as useful—in fact one for wood and another for metal are found in the best conducted shops.

That owl ? He's there to keep mice away.